3-4-6c

mississippi workers:

where they come from
and how they perform

a study of working forces
in selected mississippi
industrial plants

b. m. wofford and t. a. kelly

sponsored by
mississippi power company
mississippi power and light company
mississippi state college
north mississippi industrial development association
tennessee valley authority

published for
the business research station,
mississippi state college
by the
university of alabama press,
university, alabama

FOREWORD

ACUTELY CONSCIOUS of the low incomes provided by an unbalanced agricultural economy, citizens in overwhelming numbers in almost every Mississippi community have been quick to welcome new industrial plants. Many cities stand ready to issue bonds under Mississippi's legislatively authorized BAWI program in order to share in the risks and financing of new or expanding local industries. Tax concessions are commonly granted along with such financial aids.

Many natural factors attractive to new industry exist in abundance in Mississippi: low cost fuel and power, a favorable climate, plentiful supplies of raw materials, established markets, an abundant labor supply, and a steadily increasing amount of industrial know-how.

As business executives study this attractive situation, the answer to one vital question is not immediately apparent. Will the Mississippi worker make a good industrial employee? If more were known about him, especially his performance under actual industrial conditions, this might well be the deciding factor in the selection of an industrial plant site.

Professors Kelly and Wofford have conducted extensive research toward shedding light upon the Mississippi worker—the influence of his farm background upon his potential training and development as an industrial employee, how good a man he is in comparison with laborers from other sections of the country, and the significant differences that may exist among various segments of the Mississippi labor force.

Although this report is one of the first attempts ever made in Mississippi to find these answers, the job has been done with a thoroughness that will contribute to a much better understanding of the Mississippi worker. The Business Research Station of Mississippi State College is happy to add this contribution to its series of studies of Mississippi's industrial growth.

ROBERT C. WEEMS, JR.
Dean of School of Business and Industry
and Director of Business Research Station

PREFACE

THIS BOOK is the result of the cooperation of a great many people. The Mississippi Power Company, the Mississippi Power and Light Company, and the North Mississippi Industrial Development Association introduced the authors to the managements of the various plants as the first step in obtaining permission to study the plants. The Tennessee Valley Authority provided technical assistance with emphasis on matters of presentation. In addition, all four of the above provided financial assistance. We obtained information on local labor market conditions from the Mississippi Employment Security Commission and advice in selecting plants from the Mississippi Agricultural and Industrial Board.

In the report which follows, Chapter I represents an attempt at a non-technical presentation of the main points of the whole project. Chapter II introduces the detailed part of the report and describes the purposes and methods of the investigation. Chapters III, IV, and V describe the plants studied and the performances of each plant working force in comparison with its non-Mississippi counterpart. Chapter VI compares the performances of various groups of workers within the Mississippi plants. Chapter VII presents the major findings of the study.

We wish to express our thanks to the multitude of people who have rendered indispensable assistance, with particular gratitude to the organizations and men who have sponsored this project, including Stefan Robock and Ernest Harvey of the Tennessee Valley Authority; L. O. Bradshaw of the Mississippi Power and Light Company; L. P. Sweatt, R. M. Shearer, and Victor Daniels of the Mississippi Power Company; Harry Clark of the North Mississippi Industrial Development Association; W. E. Barksdale and his staff of the Agricultural and Industrial Board; and P. L. Rainwater and his staff of the Research and Statistics Section of the Mississippi Employment Security Commission. This report would have been impossible without the fullest cooperation of the representatives of the plants studied. For this indispensable cooperation we are deeply indebted to C. B. Rutledge and Gilbert Twyman of Mississippi Products, Inc.; Duane Shields, William McMillan, and Polly Lacey of the Southern Division of the Superior Coach Corporation; and O. C. Klingsick and C. R. Godwin of Day-Brite Lighting, Inc.

Much of the routine conected with this project fell into the hands of a long line of student assistants whose services were invaluable. They included Frances Bethany, Gyles Eaves, Bobbie Lou Bradshaw, Mr. and Mrs. Gilbert Slater, William T. Tucker, Mr. and Mrs. Robert F. Graves, and Juanita Messer. But this was not the extent of the assistance obtained from the staff of Mississippi State College. Thanks are due Robert Holland, associate professor of English, who edited the entire report and helped with the preparation of Chapter One. The authors are also grateful to the following, who assisted in reading the manuscript and made innumerable suggestions for improvement: Alan Dailey, Norman E. Weir, and John K. Bettersworth.

Gratitude is hereby expressed to the Board of Trustees of Institutions of Higher Learning for their token of confidence in the form of a research grant to allow this work to be carried on.

Finally, the authors wish to express their thanks for invaluable advice and active support to R. C. Weems, Dean of the School of Business and Industry, and Director of the Business Research Station, Mississippi State College.

B. M. WOFFORD
T. A. KELLY

September, 1954

CONTENTS

TABLE OF CHARTS

I

INTRODUCTION: A BRIEF LOOK AT THE STUDY AND ITS CONCLUSIONS

H OW GOOD is the Mississippi laborer as an industrial worker? Does he compare favorably or unfavorably with the industrial worker in other sections of the country? In Mississippi, where industrialism is beginning to achieve full stature, is the primarily agricultural-minded Mississippi worker able to adjust satisfactorily to industrial conditions and demands? From the standpoint of its manpower, is the South a good field for industrial development? Will the prospective industrial manager, moving South, find in this region a satisfactory or an unsatisfactory manpower situation? Are only certain Mississippians able to become satisfactory industrial workers? Have present employers skimmed the cream off the potential industrial labor force? Has the supply of the kinds of Mississippians who make good industrial employees been exhausted or do all kinds of Mississippians represent potential successful industrial employees? Is the Southern Negro, as well as the Southern white man, an industrial employee of good potential? Is there a difference in adaptability to the industrial environment between the urban and the rural Mississippian, the educated and the uneducated, the younger and the older, the worker with a farming background and the worker with manufacturing experience?

In order to get at least a partial answer to these questions, this study was made of three industrial plants in the State of Mississippi:

1. Mississippi Products, Inc., of Jackson. Established in 1946 as a subsidiary of Sears, Roebuck and Company, Mississippi Products is engaged in the manufacture of furniture. It is not a BAWI[1] plant.
2. Day-Brite Lighting, Inc., of Tupelo, a BAWI plant opened in 1947 and engaged in the manufacture of fluorescent lighting fixtures.
3. Pathfinder Coach Division of Superior Coaches, Inc., (Lima, Ohio), of Kosciusko. A BAWI plant manufacturing bus bodies principally. It was opened in 1951.

The labor supply in these plants was first evaluated from the standpoint of its availability. The conclusion is that in all cases the labor

---

[1]Mississippi's Balance Agriculture with Industry plan, the official state program for the encouragement of new industries in the state.

forces were found with ease. Though the time of hiring was during
the immediate postwar years, the suggestion is that Mississippi, and
probably the South, for a long time to come will have a great reservoir
of labor for industrial uses.

Next, the labor in these three plants was evaluated in comparison
with labor in comparable plants outside Mississippi and with the national average in like industries. Finally, the labor forces of these
plants were studied on the basis of group characteristics, such as age,
race, education, former occupation, and rural and urban background.
The comparison of Mississippi with non-Mississippi workers serves to
evaluate the relative fitness of native Mississippi labor in industrial
work; the group characteristic comparisons will serve employers in
choosing among various segments of the local labor population.

In the comparisons between the labor performances of the Mississippi and the non-Mississippi plants, it was found that Mississippi
labor as a whole favorably compares with that of other sections. (The
specific comparisons were made between Mississippi Products, Inc.,
and a plant in Kentucky; between the Pathfinder Coach Division at
Kosciusko and the parent plant at Lima, Ohio; between Day-Brite
Lighting, Inc., and a plant in St. Louis. While these plants of comparison are not all Northern plants, they are all in regions more
heavily industrialized than Mississippi and more oriented toward the
industrial environment. General comparisons were made between the
three Mississippi plants and industries as a whole, nationwide, through
the use of Bureau of Labor Statistics.) In general the comparison
studies show that the absentee rate of Mississippi workers is not high
in comparison with that of non-Mississippi workers. Mississippi labor,
in other words, can be depended on to man the industrial plants regularly. Even more in favor of the Mississippi labor force, it was found
that, after the breaking-in period, the Mississippi rate of turnover is
somewhat lower than the average for the nation in similar industries.
Perhaps these two findings together suggest that the picture of the
typical Southerner as a shiftless ne'er-do-well is more myth than
reality. Another comparison between the Mississippi and the non-
Mississippi worker was made on the basis of frequency and severity of
accidents, a matter of significance in both human and financial terms
to both labor and management. In comparison with the national average, the study shows that, except for the breaking-in period, the
Mississippi record in both accident categories (frequency and severity)

is better than that of the nation. Finally, from the standpoint of productiveness, it was found that the output of Mississippi and non-Mississippi workers in similar jobs is about the same. Taken as a whole, the study shows that Mississippi labor holds its own, in spite of the lack of an industrial tradition (and perhaps some people might think because of such a lack) with labor from other sections of the country.

Turning from the regional comparisons to comparisons within the native Mississippi labor force itself, some interesting conclusions were found, although in general none of the characteristic groups was found to be superior to the others. The method used for this characteristic group check was to categorize the labor force into sex, race, education, rural or urban background, occupational history, and such groups, and to check each of them for such ratings as absenteeism, separations exclusive of layoffs (quitting the job), output, promotional progress, and layoffs.

The records show that the Mississippi Negro was less absent than his white co-worker and that he had a lower rate of separations exclusive of layoffs. In output, though this comparison was difficult to make because the cases were few in which the Negro and the white man worked at the same job, he showed about the same standard as the white worker. Somewhat at odds with these findings favoring the Negro worker was the layoff rate, which favored the white. This difference, however, is probably a reflection of factors which go beyond the efficiency or the inefficiency of the workers involved. Broad sociological studies could be made on this discrepancy. It is encouraging that the Negroes, who form such a numerical mass of the Mississippi population, are evidently entirely capable in industrial work.

In the age group study, it was found that the results favored the older workers in rates of absence, separations exclusive of layoffs, and layoffs. On the other hand, the younger employees achieved greater promotional progress. The conclusion seems to be about what one would expect: that the older worker is steadier, more conscientious, and more dependable, but that the younger is more apt, more alert on the job, and of more potential value to the employer than the older man. This conclusion seems to follow especially from the fact that in output there was no superiority indicated for either group.

The median number of years of school completed by the adult popu-

lation in the South is consistently reported by the Bureau of Census
as lower than in other sections of the nation. In the plants included
in this study, management established certain educational qualifications for employment. The result was that the median education of
employees in these plants was higher than that of the adult population in the local labor market areas. However, the workers with more
schooling did not represent the "cream of the crop" with respect to
good performance on the job. Instead, the study of the educational
backgrounds of the workers in these three plants and the performances
of the various educational groups shows that those workers with less
education are less frequently absent from the job and that they achieve
greater promotional progress in the semi-skilled levels. The better
educated, however, show a more favorable separation rate exclusive
of layoffs than the less educated. The output of workers in the two
categories is about the same. Since the jobs tested in this study were
all below administrative level, the educational conclusions mean only
that education seems to be of no great advantage to the vocational
or mechanical worker at his work, as measured against the standard
listed above.

Workers with rural backgrounds made a better showing than those
of urban background in absence rates, separation rates exclusive of
layoff, and promotional progress both skilled and semi-skilled. The
only phase in which the urban worker was favored was in the layoff
rate, which like the Negro-white situation described above is a reflection of employer opinion and not necessarily an accurate measure
of the worth of the worker. It suggests that the industrial manager
quite often makes the human error of operating on assumptions rather
than on established facts.

Somewhat similar to the rural-urban comparison was the comparison between those with manufacturing experience and those with
farming experience as occupational background. The manufacturing
experience worker had a better absentee record than the farming experience employee, but he had a higher rate of turnover exclusive of
layoffs. There was little difference between the promotional records
of these two groups, and that little favored the worker with farming
experience. The technically trained worker was absent less often and
produced better than the non-technically trained, as was to be
expected.

Finally, it was found that married men were more steadily on the job than were their more footloose bachelor co-workers, and that the married worker produced better. Though otherwise there was little difference between the categories, it seems established that the married man is in general a better bet than the unmarried at settled and regular work.

The above, then, are a few of the principal conclusions of the following study. It is hoped that it will be of profit to the industrialist contemplating establishment in the South, to the manager already on the ground, to businessmen and financiers, to mayors and students.

II

HOW THE STUDY WAS DONE

1. THE PROBLEM OF LOW INCOMES

WHETHER ONE VIEWS the South as the nation's number one economic problem[1] or as the nation's number one economic opportunity, the low average income of Southerners is an established fact.

The South and particularly Mississippi are at or near the bottom of almost every statistical series which meaures income. Not only does this reflect a low level of living, but it implies many attendant evils.

The high fertility of the Southern population commits the South to train almost one-third of the nation's children on approximately one-sixth of the nation's school expenditures.

Another shortcoming of the Southern economy has been a relatively extensive use of manpower in industries which employ a minimum of capital. This has meant continued low income, which has in turn made more difficult the obtaining of additional capital equipment— the typical problem of economically backward areas.

Still within the memory of most Mississippians are the disastrous effects upon health which resulted from low incomes. Pellagra, dysentery, and hookworm have in years past rendered the Southern agricultural and industrial worker less productive than his Northern neighbors.

During the last decade the situation has become more hopeful. Incomes of Southerners and especially Mississippians have been gaining at a more rapid rate than those of the nation as a whole. Several factors have been responsible for this change. Most of them are fundamental in nature, and probably all the elements are now present for the continued, rapid closing of the income gap. Southern agriculture, which suffered so severely during the depression of the 1930's, has benefited tremendously from the increase in demand which arose during the war and postwar years. As a result of heavy farm-to-town migration, the introduction of farm mechanization, and an improve-

[1]National Emergency Council, *Report on Economic Conditions of the South* (Washington: Government Printing Office, 1938), p. 1.

ment in the breeding of crops and animals, the value of farm produce rose at the same time that the number of people engaged in farming declined. In addition the government has offered the farmer the opportunity to participate in price control measures designed to insure him against another drop in his income.

The improvements in income, which have been made in the last twenty years combined with advancements in public health and medical knowledge, have rendered diseases of poverty less enervating than in the past. The table on page 8 shows the record from 1937 through 1951 of deaths from four selected debilitating diseases and the total number of cases of these diseases reported for Mississippi.[2] No longer do malaria, pellagra, dysentery, and hookworm have an important detrimental effect upon the people.

Also there has been a growth in the degree of industrialization of the South. As great as has been the increase between 1940 and 1950 in agricultural and other non-manufacturing incomes in Mississippi (206% and 258% respectively), manufacturing payrolls have grown even faster (284%).[3]

Mississippi still has the lowest per capita income of all the Southern states, and this situation is receiving increased attention both within the State and from outsiders interested in the national welfare. The solution of Mississippi's economic problem would benefit not only the people of the State but also those of the South and of the nation. However, the South has not yet caught up with the rest of the nation, and the per capita incomes of its states are still among the lowest in the union. A more productive South would increase the economic strength of the nation. In time of war, military strength depends on economic strength, and a highly productive South with its strategically defensible location would add materially to national security. An increase in the standard of living of the people of the South would, in time of war or peace, provide increased markets for the goods produced by our highly efficient national economy and thereby would play a part in preventing business recessions.

It is logical that Mississippi, having been more heavily afflicted with the typically Southern economic ills than any other state, should

[2]The drop in incidence from 1946 to 1947 is explained in part by a change in the system of reporting to require a proof of diagnosis in cases of malaria, pellagra, and dysentery.

[3]*Survey of Current Business*, XXXI (August, 1951), 14, 15.

DEATHS* | **NUMBER OF CASES REPORTED****

YEAR	PELLAGRA	MALARIA	DYSENTERY	HOOKWORM	PELLAGRA	MALARIA	DYSENTERY	HOOKWORM
1937	234	312	120	1	3,698	47,883	10,769	5,197
1938	267	275	145	2	5,193	44,346	11,104	6,448
1939	197	235	126	2	4,428	44,422	11,364	7,240
1940	169	174	138	.	4,139	41,237	11,625	7,248
1941	121	150	151	1	2,873	36,815	12,445	7,901
1942	117	79	111	0	3,313	31,752	13,619	6,355
1943	82	67	79	2	2,752	25,094	13,550	4,975
1944	66	63	76	1	2,564	23,133	12,975	5,022
1945	56	37	36	1	2,077	18,860	11,199	5,057
1946	45	29	28	0	2,091	17,764	8,651	5,116
1947	30	20	29	1	18	877	236	1,943
1948	29	10	30	0	40	125	319	3,204
1949	18	5	64	1	44	75	251	3,309
1950	16	2	39	.	29	64	195	3,059
1951	11	1	64	2	13	46	254	2,540

*U. S. Public Health Service, *Vital Statistics of the U. S.,* "Deaths from Selected Causes, Mississippi," 1937-1951.

**State Board of Health Biennial Reports, "Cases of Diseases."

have shown great improvement during the past decade. The need is to see that this trend continues at an accelerated pace. Given a continuation of high national prosperity, the continued improvement of agricultural incomes seems assured. The flood of new chemicals for farm use promises tremendous advancement in soil conditioning, insect control, weed eradication, and fertilization. The development of specialized machines will end forever the farm technology based on "forty acres and a mule." King Cotton, while still a royal monarch, is being forced to yield more and more of his sovereignty to general farming, animal husbandry, and timber crops. The research divisions of the state and national governments are bringing forth new agricultural wonders which are being passed on to farm operators through an efficient system of county agents and home demonstration agents. New techniques of food preservation are enriching the rural diet and opening vast new markets for farm produce. During the past decade the diets of the people of the United States have improved, and there is every indication that they will continue to improve in the future. The influence of all these changes is now felt, and the end does not appear to be in sight. Only a business recession seems to be a possible bar to the continued increase in the level of agricultural income.

2. DESIRABILITY OF A FURTHER SHIFT OF AGRICULTURAL WORKERS INTO NON-AGRICULTURAL JOBS

Despite all the improvement in the condition of the farmer, agriculture continues to be, relatively, a low-income occupation.[4] If the State as a whole is to enjoy maximum benefits, to increase employment opportunities, and to maximize the average productivity of Mississippi workers, means must be provided which will allow workers to shift from agriculture to other industries where the value added to the product is greater for each man-hour of labor utilized.

The extent to which the economic welfare of Mississippi can be improved through industrialization will depend on how well its resources can be industrially adapted. Mississippi has many resources: much of its agricultural land is highly productive, its mineral resources are considerable, and its climate is well suited to a large variety of occupations. In addition, and high on the list in relative

---

[4]*Survey of Current Business,* XXXI (August, 1951), 14.

importance, is manpower. In determining the capacity of Mississippi
to accept industrialization, the suitability of its manpower for industrial employment may be decisive.

In periods of high national income, abundant and suitable manpower might be a causative factor in the industrialization of Mississippi. Considerable doubt has arisen since the beginning of World
War II as to the desirability of moving labor to predetermined industrial locations with all the attendant difficulties inherent in this procedure, and more thought is being devoted to the possibility of the
location of industry in such a manner as to minimize the dislocation
of families. In periods of slack employment an efficient working force
would be a prerequisite to continued industrialization. In such times,
considerations of trainability and productivity might be decisive in
determining location of new industrial plants and the continued operation of existing plants. To the end that optimum occupational distribution for Mississippians may be estimated, all information concerning the industrial capacity of the workers of this state will serve
a useful purpose.

3. IS INDUSTRIALIZATION A SOLUTION?

With the above considerations in mind, it was the purpose of this
study to obtain objective, factual information concerning the adaptability of Mississippi people to industrial employment. To accomplish
this purpose, it was necessary to compare productivity in Mississippi
plants and in plants located in other regions, and to compare the relative efficiency of different groups of Mississippi workers with different
personal characteristics. If Mississippi is to be further industrialized,
it must be shown that, in addition to having successfully accomplished
the task of manning present industrial plants, the State will be likely
to have available for future plants an effectively producing labor force.
That is to say, have all of the Mississippians of the kind likely to make
successful industrial employees been employed in the industries already established in the State, so that future employers will not be
able to man their plants as successfully? Or are many of the different
characteristic groups to be found in Mississippi potentially desirable
industrial employees? For instance, do Negroes make good workers of
this kind? What about the older Mississippians, the less educated,
those with little or no experience outside farming? If all these, and
other such people, can shift successfully to industrial employment,

then Mississippi may well be able to man an extensive program of industrialization. It was also felt that an account of the performance of several hundred Mississippi production workers in the environment of up-to-date industrial plants would be of interest to prospective employers and others in a position to influence the future rate of industrial growth in the State.

4. EXPERIENCES OF SELECTED PLANTS

The case study method was used here because it was thought that this method could develop as much information as could be obtained on the subject within the limits of the funds available. Since the chief interest was in the labor force available for the future, on which prewar experience would shed little light, the cases chosen for study were plants which had recruited their working forces since World War II. The whole environment in which labor is now recruited differs radically from that of the prewar years. War, and the labor shortage, have added greatly to the dignity of labor. In addition, the greater availability of records of labor recruitments since the war makes a study of this kind more likely to be accurate and meaningful. The cases also were to include data showing variety in products, skill requirements, size of plant, geographical location (within the State), and size of community. Plants were chosen which belonged to concerns having plants in other regions producing the same sort of product under similar conditions. Within these limits the plants were selected arbitrarily with a view to providing information about the kind of industry which Mississippi could use to raise the standard of living.

The data gathered included information by which labor efficiency in Mississippi plants could be compared with that found in non-Mississippi plants: absentee records, data on turnover, information concerning the frequency and severity of accidents, and man-hours required in Mississippi plants to produce certain units of output as compared with the number of man-hours required in non-Mississippi plants to procure the same unit of output with the same types of equipment. Data were gathered for the productive labor forces on the following characteristics:

1. Age
2. Race
3. Sex

4. Marital status
5. Education
6. Technical training
7. Place of birth
8. Place of residence before taking job
9. Present residence
10. Employment status before taking job
11. Occupational history

This information on personal characteristics was obtained from applications for employment prepared by the personnel departments. Age was sometimes checked by cross reference to date of birth, but usually the applicant's statement of age was accepted. The data on education were accepted as written, although this might be considered a prestige question.

Estimating trainability involved a measure of the time required by each employee in certain job classifications to attain a satisfactory standard speed of production. Further information on this point was obtained by a comparison of the length of time required for promotion from one job to another involving a higher type of skill as defined by management. In certain job classifications, where records were kept on individual output and where the rate of output depended on the individual and not on the speed of the machine or on speed of fellow workers, data as to number of units produced per hour (or man-hours per unit) were gathered. Computations of the average output of all individuals in each classification were made. The output of each characteristic group, a group of people having one or more designated characteristics in common, such as male employees without manufacturing experience, was compared with the average for all workers in the same job classification in order to evaluate the degree of success attained by persons having these characteristics.

The average number of days absent per year (from causes beyond the control of the employer) was computed for each individual, averages for the whole group were found, and the averages for each characteristic group were compared to discover any meaningful differences in job attendance. Average turnover rates were computed, and the average turnover for each of the characteristic groups was shown in order to reveal any characteristic group which differed substantially.

If it is revealed that the present degree of success of Mississippians in industrial employment is the result of highly selective hiring of workers, then the degree of future industrialization possible is greatly reduced. If, on the other hand, the hiring and the successful training of the labor forces involves a material cross-section of the whole population, the limit to which the State may be industrialized is increased.

In an attempt to discover whether we are dealing with a selected group of workers or with the entire Mississippi labor force, various characteristics of the individuals employed have been used. It is entirely possible, however, that these characteristics did not include all of those which would be of importance in determining success in industrial employment. There may be other characteristics, unmeasured in this study, which would account to a greater degree for success in adjustment to industrial environment. Also, this study does not rule out the possibility that that portion of the population which has shifted to industrial employment is not characteristic of the entire population. These limitations are not inherent characteristics of the case study method, but would also be present even when a probability sample was employed. This fact, together with the considerably greater expense and personnel requirements of the probability sample method, led to the adoption of the case study method.

Statistical significance measures were not deemed suitable for these data. Instead, descriptive measures were used to portray the size and the degree of consistency of the difference in performance of the various characteristic groups from plant to plant. Variations in processes, skill requirements, personnel policies, and wage systems precluded the pooling of data for all three plants.

The possibility of inter-correlations between several performance measures taken from the same group of people was recognized. However, the usual simultaneous multi-variable analysis could not be used with these data, since most of the groups were classified qualitatively rather than quantitatively, and similar methods for qualitative data[5] would have added excessively to the expense and time required to complete the study.

---

[5]*E.g.*, the successive approximation method presented in Chapter 17 of Mordecai Ezekiel, *Methods of Correlation Analysis* (New York: John Wiley & Sons, 1941).

III

THE CASE OF "MISSISSIPPI PRODUCTS"

1. AVAILABILITY OF LABOR

Since the technique here in use was the case study method, the generalizations which might be drawn will be applicable only to cases that differ in no important degree from the case under consideration. To evaluate fully the availability of labor, then, it was necessary to describe the company, the labor market as it existed at that time, the working conditions offered in the market, and, finally, the labor force which was employed.

The Labor Market. The Mississippi Products, Inc., plant is located on the outskirts of the City of Jackson, the capital and the largest city in Mississippi. Jackson increased in population from 62,107 in 1940 to 97,674 in 1950.[1] Business activity in the city more than tripled during this period in terms of dollars and more than doubled in physical volume, as indicated in the following table:

NON-DEFLATED AND DEFLATED INDEXES OF BUSINESS ACTIVITY
IN JACKSON 1940-1950* (1930-1940 = 100)

YEAR	NON-DEFLATED INDEX	DEFLATED INDEX
1940	104	104
1941	122	114
1942	150	128
1943	180	149
1944	195	140
1945	213	175
1946	233	173
1947	273	175
1948	316	191
1949	327	205
1950	362	226

*William Weiner, "Twelve Years of Business Activity in the City of Jackson, 1939-1950," *Mississippi Business Review,* XII (March, 1951), 16.

[1] United States Bureau of the Census, *Census of Population: 1950* (Washington: Government Printing Office, 1952), I, 24-27.

Since the end of World War II, 53 manufacturing plants employing eight or more persons have been established in the Jackson area (Hinds County).

Mississippi Products, Inc., began hiring production workers in 1946 and stepped up the rate of hiring in 1947, a period when the supply of available labor was relatively plentiful in the Jackson area.

Unemployment in Hinds County at this time, as estimated by the Mississippi Employment Security Commission, was reported as follows:*

MONTH AND YEAR	ESTIMATED UNEMPLOYMENT
1947	
January	4,200
March	3,600
May	3,300
July	3,600
September	2,200
November	1,950
1948	
January	2,400
March	2,750
May	2,500
July	2,550
September	1,200

*Mississippi Employment Security Commission, "Form ES 274," February, 1947, to October, 1948, inclusive, from the files of the Jackson Office.

The Mississippi Employment Security Commission reported, in a survey of both covered and non-covered workers that "employment in all manufacturing groups except lumber and wood products and furniture and fixtures dropped off in varying proportions (in 1947)."[2]

In addition to these workers made available because firms that would normally be competing buyers of local labor reduced their employment, the labor supply available to Mississippi Products, Inc., was further increased by an influx of women into the labor market. According to the report, "progressive increases in the cost of living had sent women into the labor market in larger numbers to supplement family earnings."[3]

[2]USES 274 "Report for the Jackson, Mississippi, Labor Market Area for February, 1948," p. 2.
[3]*Ibid.*, p. 5.

The company confined its recruitment program to workers available locally and within a 35-mile commuting radius. Early in 1948, the Mississippi Employment Service reported: "The principal barrier to recruitment from outside the area is the scarcity of housing. Considerable construction of dwelling units is under way, or scheduled, but it is unlikely that 1949 completions will adequately house the present population."[4]

This situation was not remedied until 1950, when housing became reasonably adequate, the Bureau of the Census reporting a vacancy rate of 3.7 per cent for non-seasonal non-dilapidated dwellings in April of that year.[5]

The Employers. Mississippi Products, Inc., established in 1946 as a subsidiary of Sears, Roebuck and Company, completed its plant building and entered production in the latter part of that year. The plant is an integrated furniture manufacturing operation, processing logs into finished furniture. It has its own sawmill (detached from the main plant), drying kiln, and veneer plant to furnish raw materials which are converted in turn into cabinets of considerable quality through the use of a great deal of mechanical equipment and a high degree of job specialization. Its principal products are wood cabinets for radios, television sets, and sewing machines. It also manufactures a line of occasional furniture. Nearly all of these products are manufactured for the parent company; however, quite a bit of work is done for outsiders. Prior to and during the war, this work was done by another Sears subsidiary, the Adler Manufacturing Company at Louisville, Kentucky, which is no longer in operation.

According to management, the company decided on the Jackson location because of the availability of raw material (95 per cent from within 75 miles of the plant), because of the adequate labor supply as revealed by a labor survey made by a firm of industrial engineers, and because of the adequacy of transportation facilities. This plant was established in Jackson without making use of the leased factory and tax exemption benefits available under the BAWI program.

The construction of the plant facilities was carried on under contract, and the first part of the plant to be equipped was that section

---

[4]*Ibid.*, p. 4.

[5]United States Bureau of the Census, *1950 Census of Housing, Jackson, Mississippi*, H-E 85 (Washington: Government Printing Office, 1951), p. 3.

engaged in the earlier processes in cabinet construction. As each department was equipped, it was manned, and production of stock for succeeding departments was begun. When the construction neared completion Mississippi Products, Inc., hired some of the construction workers from the building contractors as production workers in the new plant.

Additional workers were obtained by application to the local office of the Mississippi Employment Security Commission, advertising in the press and on the radio, and word-of-mouth advertising on the part of the newly-employed people. No difficulty was encountered in securing the desired number of workers. As a matter of fact, according to Mr. C. B. Rutledge, personnel manager of the plant, there were during this period approximately five colored and three white applicants for each available job. However, turnover was great, perhaps because of the then prevalent restlessness in the labor supply and the unavailability of workers accustomed to the conditions of industrial employment of this kind.

The specifications set up by the management to determine the acceptability of applicants for jobs were good health and age between twenty and forty. Younger persons were considered to be unstable and people over forty generally were not considered trainable. The number of applicants meeting these qualifications was greater than the number of jobs open. Consequently the specifications were not relaxed. After 1946 the problem of hiring became easier. Mr. Rutledge reported that for each job opening for white males there were by 1951 about five applicants, for each job opening for colored males about ten applicants, and for each job opening for white females about ten applicants.

The plant employed, as production workers, white men, a few white women, and colored men. Colored women were used only in custodial capacities. Most of the hiring was done in either skill level 7 (the lowest level) or skill level 6 (the next lowest level). The lowest entering pay rate for trainees in 1946 was 55 cents per hour, though most of the hiring of trainee machine operators was done in skill level 6 at 60 cents per hour. By 1951, the starting rate for skill level 7 had increased to 88½ cents and the starting rate for skill level 6 had increased to 94 cents. In the beginning, the whole plant was operated as a training unit, under the supervision of approximately sixty supervisors, technical men, and managers brought to Jackson from

Louisville. All production workers, including the most highly skilled, were hired and trained locally.

The general wage policy of the company was summed up by the plant management as the payment of wages equal to or better than those paid by like industries in the area. The cost of living was taken into account only to the extent that competitors in the labor market made such adjustments. A 5-cent to 6-cent increase was given each worker who completed 24 weeks of satisfactory service. The company had, in addition, by the time of this study, certain fringe benefits. An employee who had been with the company one year was eligible for sick leave pay of $25 per week for three weeks after a waiting period of one week. After two years, eight weeks' benefits could be received, and after five years a maximum of ten weeks' benefits. The company also carried the hospital and surgical insurance plan of the parent corporation, Sears, Roebuck and Company, which provided hospital and surgical benefits to the worker and his family. This was a voluntary program, toward which the workers paid 75 cents per week; the company paid the rest, which was estimated to be at least an additional 75 cents per week. Plans of group life insurance and retirement benefits were also provided. Of these plans the company said: "Life insurance is provided under the Sears group contract at 50 cents per $1000 of coverage per month. Employees also are members of the famous Savings and Profit-Sharing Pension Fund of Sears, Roebuck and Company Employees, through which employees acquire a proprietary interest in the company with the purchase of Sears stock from a share in the company profits each year."[6] A suggestion system was installed in 1948, under which employees making cost-reducing suggestions were eligible to receive 50 per cent of the savings resulting from the adoption of their suggestions (less tooling costs) during the first year up to a maximum of $500.

The company made wide use of both individual and group incentive plans, under a system introduced gradually during the first three years of operation. In August, 1951, a low point in employment, there were 235 production employees on individual incentive rates, 208 on group incentive rates, and 200 on time pay.

The company also supported certain recreational activities aimed at improving employee relations. For both male and female employees

[6]Quoted from a letter from Mr. C. B. Rutledge, Personnel Manager, to the authors.

there were softball teams, basketball teams, and a monthly prize for the largest fish caught. A house organ was published bi-weekly.

The workers of the plant were not represented by a union in bargaining with management. An organization drive in 1948 by the International Woodworkers of America, CIO, and the United Brotherhood of Carpenters and Joiners of America, AFL, was followed by a National Labor Relations Board representation election in August, 1948. In this election 366 votes were cast for the International Woodworkers, 28 for the United Brotherhood of Carpenters and Joiners, and 463 for no union representation.

The Workers. In the labor market described above, Mississippi Products, Inc., was able to hire what management considered to be a highly satisfactory labor force. President G. A. Huth wrote:

We have found that the Jackson working man or woman is much more cooperative with management than his counterpart in many northern and eastern cities. In most instances he has not been subjected to socialistic and other radical thinking nor to the anti-management propaganda of the unions.

The cooperative spirit of our employees combined with their willingness to work and their eagerness to learn has provided us with an efficient and productive work force.

MPI people are confident of their craftsmanship and proud of their product. In the short 5-year period of MPI's history they have developed into as skilled a group of cabinet workers as can be found in any factory in the country.

That old saw about the non-productiveness and low skill of the southern worker has been put to rest once and for all at the MPI. We use incentive in our plant and MPI'ers have developed incentive mindedness and an incentive pace better than that of the work force at our former Adler Manufacturing Company operation at Louisville, Kentucky. Our 40 odd supervisors who transferred from the Louisville plant are unanimous in their expert opinion on this point which is borne out by a comparison of the incentive earnings records of the two plants.

Much has been said about the unsuitability of the southern negro for industrial life. At MPI, to be sure, the Jackson negro usually learns a new job more slowly than the white man, which is mostly due to lack of self-confidence. But we have found that with the proper training and handling, his turnover rate, his absentee rate, his productivity and workmanship have been excellent.[7]

[7]Letter from G. A. Huth, President of Mississippi Products, Inc., to Wendell Black, General Manager of the Jackson Chamber of Commerce, September 11, 1951.

Employment of production workers in the plant, since the beginning of operations in 1947, averaged as follows:

	White Males		White Females		Colored Males		
Year	No.	Per Cent	No.	Per Cent	No.	Per Cent	Total
1947	358	48	73	10	310	42	741
1948	375	44	78	9	409	47	862
1949	321	45	59	8	341	47	721
1950	543	44	82	7	614	49	1,239
1951	388	43	68	8	433	49	889

The use of Negroes as production workers in plants of this kind is relatively new in the South. In the first four years of the plant's operation, there was an increase in the proportion of Negroes among the production workers, but this was no longer true as of August, 1951.

2. TRAINABILITY

Training Program. In many industries the cost of training new employees represents a sizeable fraction of total production cost, especially when labor turnover is high. In some occupations it has been found expedient to hire special instructors and to set aside space and equipment to be devoted exclusively to training. After an initial period in 1946, when the whole plant was used as a training department, Mississippi Products, Inc., did not find it necessary to make any special provision for training its production workers outside the space regularly used in day-to-day production. The extent to which job specialization was used reduced the learning task faced by most new production workers, so that instruction by the foreman and by selected employee trainers on the job was a sufficient training program. Some of the more skilled workers, maintenance men and craftsmen, were trained in the plant. Other positions of skill were filled by persons who got their training elsewhere.

The Learning Period. The establishment of the training period for newly-hired workers in this plant was made difficult by the absence of records concerning output during the first few days of employment.

When a worker was hired, he was assigned as an observer to some trained workman. After a time, he took over the operation of the machine, with the trained worker acting as an observer and instructor. During this time, which usually varied from three to five days, neither the new worker nor the instructor was on the incentive plan, and therefore no record was kept of the pieces produced. At the end of the observation period, the new worker took over the operation of the machine and went on the incentive plan, though it was understood that his production might be less than the standard for the job. If his production was below standard, his earnings were increased so as to make them equal to what they would have been if he had produced at the standard rate. It should be noted that the production of the average worker working at normal speed was expected by the company to average 25 per cent more than standard production.

Records, then, were available on the output of the worker following the observation period, and a study of these records gave some idea of the rapidity of the learning process. Data were gathered on ninety workers employed for the first time during the spring of 1952, and a determination was made as to whether or not the worker attained standard during the first five working days subsequent to the observation period. The following table shows the fraction of these ninety workers who achieved standard for at least one day, classified according to the number of days of independent experience the worker had had prior to such achievement of standard:

Days of Independent Experience Before Making Standard	Number of Workers	Per Cent of Workers	Cumulative Per Cents
0	21	23.3	23.3
1	17	18.9	42.2
2	11	12.2	54.4
3	8	8.9	63.3
4	7	7.8	71.1
5	4	4.4	75.5
Over 5	22	24.4	100.0

An alternative criterion considered was that of the achievement of standard for two days in succession. The number of days of prior independent experience necessary for this achievement and the percentage of workers who attained it after the varying amounts of experience are shown in the following table:

DAYS OF INDEPENDENT EXPERIENCE	NUMBER OF WORKERS	PER CENT OF WORKERS	CUMULATIVE PER CENTS
0	12	13.6	13.6
1	12	13.6	27.2
2	9	10.2	37.4
3	4	4.5	41.9
4	5	5.7	47.6
5	2	2.3	49.9
Over 5	44	50.0	100.0

The same information is indicated in Chart 1.

3. LABOR EFFICIENCY: MISSISSIPPI VERSUS NON-MISSISSIPPI

Absenteeism. Irregular attendance, or high absentee rates, cannot be tolerated in an industrial plant if a high rate of production per man-hour is to be achieved. One of the accusations often made against Southern labor is that rural Southerners will not accept the stricter discipline of industrial plants, that they have been habituated to a much wider freedom of choice as to the activity to be engaged in on a particular day, and that as a result they are undependable as industrial workers because of sporadic attendance. For these reasons it was felt that data on this matter would be indicative of the success with which Mississippi workers had adapted themselves to industrial employment. The following table shows the average per cent of workers absent per working day for the current labor force at Mississippi Products, Inc., for each of the years from 1947 to 1951.

YEAR	AVERAGE PER CENT ABSENCES
1947	5.01
1948	4.05
1949	2.07
1950	2.30
1951	1.70

CHART 1.

Days of Independent Experience Before Making Standard
Production for One Day

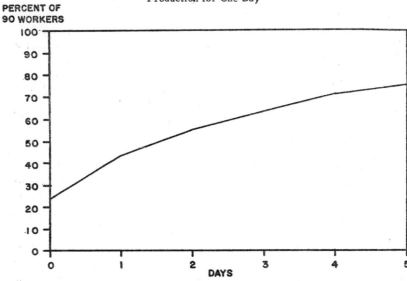

Days of Independent Experience Before Making Standard
Production for Two Successive Days

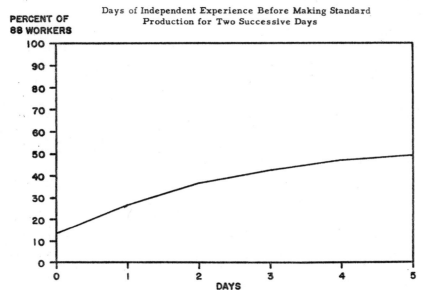

An attempt was made to discover the absentee experience of comparable plants in other sections of the country as a basis for evaluating the above figures. It appeared, however, that the wartime concern over absenteeism had declined in the postwar period to such an extent that published data on this matter were not available for the last few years. The latest data available were for 109 manufacturing plants in 1947 as reported in the *Monthly Labor Review*. These showed that the rates were: 3.2 per cent for men, 6.5 per cent for women, and 3.4 per cent for all workers.[8]

These annual averages concealed much of the detail which became apparent when the data were broken down by accounting periods, of which there were thirteen of four weeks' duration in the Mississippi Products, Inc., plant records. Chart 2 shows the average per cent of workers absent per working day for each accounting period, together with a second-degree trend fitted by the method of least-squares to this five-year period. Attention is called to the sharp downward slope in the trend line, as the average per cent absenteeism declined from 5.0 per cent in 1947 to 1.7 per cent in 1951.

The seasonal variation in absenteeism was investigated by computing deviations for each accounting period from this trend line. These deviations proved to be highly erratic, indicating little consistency in the seasonal pattern. Median deviations for each accounting period showed a tendency for absenteeism to rise to slight seasonal peaks in February and late summer with a seasonal low in the fall. These calculations are shown graphically in Chart 3. This pattern ran counter to that of the seasonal variation in agricultural employment in the South. Thus the slight evidence of seasonal variation in absenteeism could not be attributed to time taken off for planting and harvesting. It seems likely that the seasonal peak in February was largely the result of illness from winter respiratory ailments. This followed the pattern established in data on illness in *Public Health Reports*.[9]

Turnover. A high rate of labor turnover has come to be recognized by management as a costly situation to be avoided if possible. When workers are constantly being replaced, efficiency has a tendency to go down because, first, the new workers must be trained, an expensive

[8]M. D. Kossoris, "Absenteeism and Injury Experience of Older Workers," *Monthly Labor Review*, LXVII (July, 1948), 16-19.

[9]Quarterly reports of national figures.

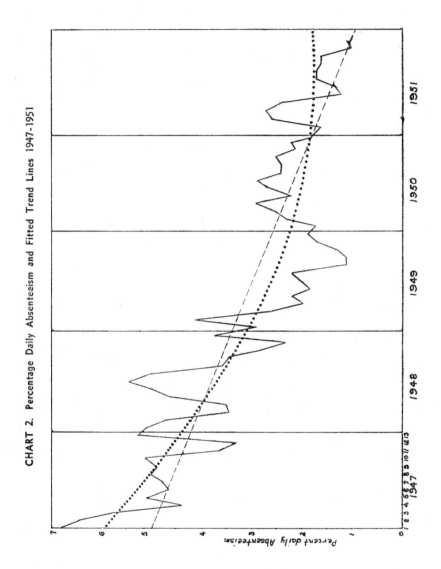

CHART 2. Percentage Daily Absenteeism and Fitted Trend Lines 1947-1951

process in itself which involves the use of facilities for training and usually a reduction in the output of old employees, and, second, because the new workers' unfamiliarity with the plant and the process prevents them, for a considerable time even after a training period, from attaining the highest rate of production of which they are

CHART 3. Deviation From Second Degree Trend Line in Average Per Cent Absenteeism

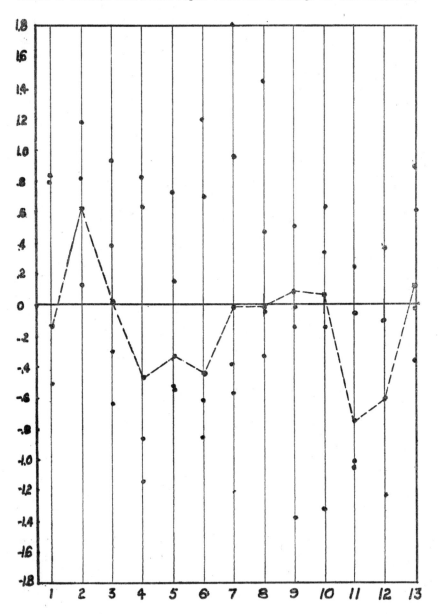

capable. Also the rate of turnover, exclusive of layoffs, is a fairly dependable measure of the mutual satisfaction of the parties in the employer-employee relationship. For this reason the figures below are presented to reflect the average rate of separations exclusive of layoffs and leaves of absence.

The manning of the Mississippi Products, Inc., plant was done right after World War II, during a period when labor had still not recovered from the restlessness of the war years and when World War II veterans were making their readjustments to civilian life. In addition, it is to be expected that the turnover rate in a new plant, which is engaged in collecting a new labor force, will be higher for a time than the rate in plants which have had several years in which to discover suitable workers, and whose labor force is composed mainly of those who have had time to try the work and have found it acceptable. As might have been expected, Mississippi Products, Inc., had a high turnover rate in the beginning, as shown in the following table comparing the rate of separation in this plant, exclusive of layoffs and leaves of absence, with the same rate for all furniture manufacturing plants included in the Bureau of Labor Statistics studies for the country as a whole.

AVERAGE MONTHLY EMPLOYEE SEPARATIONS EXCLUSIVE OF LAYOFFS
(per 100 employees)

YEAR	MISS. PRODUCTS INC.	FURNITURE* MFG. U. S.
1947	12.90	6.0
1948	6.73	5.0
1949	3.09	2.8
1950	3.43	4.4
1951	3.25	4.5

*Figures for 1947, 1948, and 1949 are for furniture industries, including manufacture of mattresses and bed springs, and figures for 1950 and 1951 are for household furniture manufacturing, as reported in the *Monthly Labor Review*, LXXV, (July, 1952), 91.

As shown above, there was a rather steep downward trend for the first three years of operation of the plant, which leveled off after the third year of operation at somewhat below the rate for all furniture manufacturing plants. This tendency is made even clearer by Chart 4,

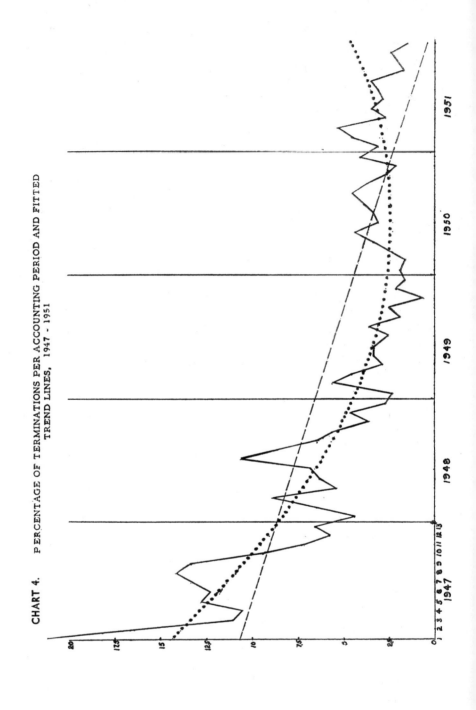

CHART 4.   PERCENTAGE OF TERMINATIONS PER ACCOUNTING PERIOD AND FITTED
TREND LINES, 1947 - 1951

CHART 5. Deviation From Second Degree Trend Line in Average Per Cent Turnover

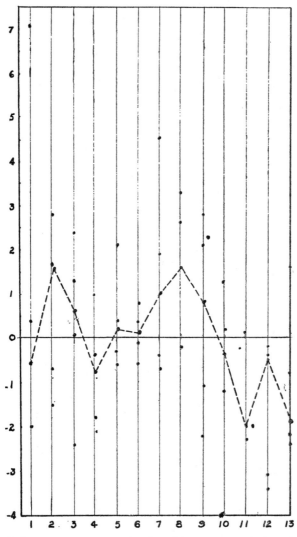

a graph of the turnover rates in the thirteen accounting periods per year, together with a second-degree trend curve fitted by the method of least-squares.

In turnover, as in absenteeism, seasonal variations were not well marked and had a tendency to be erratic. The median deviations

showed a low point in January, a peak in February, a low point in
early spring, a peak in mid-summer, and low points in October and
December. This was contrary to the pattern that would be expected
if the competition of available agricultural employment were important in causing labor turnover in this plant. It may be that the
high temperatures involved in some of the processes were related to
the mid-summer peaks in absenteeism and in labor turnover.

Safety. One of the measures of a successful adaptation to the industrial environment is the capacity of a worker to produce with a minimum of injuries to himself or the workers about him. The following
table shows the frequency of injuries at Mississippi Products, Inc., per
million man-hours of work as compared to the figure released by the
Bureau of Labor Statistics for the furniture industry (except metal
furniture) of the United States:

INJURY FREQUENCY RATES

YEAR	MISSISSIPPI PRODUCTS, INC.	FURNITURE MFG., U. S.*
1947	28.9	28.2
1948	14.0	23.8
1949	18.6	22.6 (20.2**)
1950	24.4	(21.0)
1951	16.3	21.8

*Injury rate reports in Bulletins Nos. 945, 975, and 1025 of the U. S. Bureau
of Labor Statistics and preliminary injury reports in the *Monthly Labor Review*
during these years.

**Revised Series

There seemed to be no well-defined trend in these data, though the
Mississippi Products, Inc., figures were lower than the national figure
in three of the five years. Apparently, the Mississippi worker was not
particularly accident-prone, though the relatively high frequency rates
in 1947 and 1950 may indicate that the inexperienced Mississippi worker was more likely to have accidents than an experienced worker, since
these were the periods of most rapid hiring during the first five years
of operation of the plant. Because of the nature of the methods used
in the production of furniture, the frequency of accidents is likely to
be relatively high.

The following table shows the number of days lost as a result of industrial accidents per thousand man-hours of work in Mississippi Products, Inc., as compared with the industry as a whole.

INJURY SEVERITY RATES

YEAR	MISSISSIPPI PRODUCTS, INC.	FURNITURE MFG., U. S.*
1947	1.34	2.1
1948	3.64	1.9
1949	.87	1.9
1950	2.86	1.5
1951	.84	1.6

*Injury reports in Bulletins Nos. 945, 975, and 1025 of the U. S. Bureau of Labor Statistics and preliminary injury reports in the *Monthly Labor Review* during these years.

These figures would seem to indicate that Mississippi labor, coming into a new working situation, was not prone to serious accident.

No particular trend is apparent in these severity rates, the erratic behavior being due to the smaller number of cases as compared with the national average. However, the Mississippi Products, Inc., figure was below the average in three out of the five years.

Output Per Man-Hour. Before the opening of Mississippi Products, Inc., the same management operated another subsidiary plant of Sears, Roebuck and Company, the Adler Manufacturing Company of Louisville, Kentucky, which produced in general the same sort of goods as the Mississippi Products, Inc. This plant was located in an important furniture manufacturing center, where experienced furniture workers were available. It was organized by the Brotherhood of Carpenters and Joiners, AFL. The Adler plant was closed shortly after the beginning of the operation of the Jackson plant.

Although the general output of both plants consisted of radio, sewing machine, and television cabinets, the high degree of styling made it difficult to find items identical enough in nearly all respects for adjustment to be made for non-identical aspects so as to get a comparison of the man-hours required to produce the same item by the same method of production. However, one cabinet was found which, with minor adjustments, could be used as a basis for comparing pro-

ductivity in the two plants. As produced by the Adler Manufacturing
Company in 1941, this was known as Model 312 sewing machine cabinet, while at Mississippi Products, Inc., in 1950 it was known as
Model 323. Below are shown the numbers of man-hours required for
producing 100 of these cabinets by departments.[10]

DEPARTMENT	312	323
Dimension Mill	32.892	34.263
Veneer Dimension	15.490	16.424
Veneer Glue	9.624	6.989
Finish Mill	52.555	30.808
Mill Cabinet	9.250	9.337
Machine Sand	13.980	14.255
Cabinet Assembly	61.891	55.021
Finish Conveyor	95.559	105.033
Rub	6.446	8.500
Trim, Oil, Pack	27.272	22.175
Total	324.959	302.805

These figures were not entirely comparable and required adjustments if they were to measure accurately the comparable output per
man-hour. (1) In its Dimension Mill, Mississippi Products, Inc., used
a machine called the Taylor Panel-Flo. Without this machine, which
was not used in the Adler plant, the man-hours required would have
been 38.802 per hundred cabinets for that department. (2) So many
differences in machines and procedure existed between the Finish
Mill Departments at the Adler plant and Mississippi Products, Inc.,
that it was impossible to make adjustments which would assure that
the resulting data were comparable. Mr. Twyman said, "The use of
special purpose machinery and straight line production on the table
line is responsible for the saving of hours in the Finish Mill."[11] For
this reason, the man-hours assigned to the Finish Mill were excluded in making the comparison. (3) The cabinet produced by the
Adler plant was rubbed only on the top, while that produced at
Mississippi Products, Inc., was rubbed on the underside of the top as
well. An adjustment was made for this difference by computing the

[10]Memorandum to G. A. Huth, President of Mississippi Products, Inc., from G.
R. Twyman, Head, Standards Dept., October 23, 1950.
[11]*Ibid.*

time that would have been required at Mississippi Products, Inc., to rub only the top of the cabinet. This adjustment reduced the rubbing time to 6.5 man-hours per hundred cabinets.

With these adjustments, the time spent producing comparable cabinets by comparable methods would have been as follows:

DEPARTMENT	312	323
Dimension Mill	32.892	38.802
Veneer Dimension	15.490	16.424
Veneer Glue	9.624	6.989
Mill Cabinet	9.250	9.337
Machine Sand	13.980	14.255
Cabinet Assembly	61.891	55.021
Finish Conveyor	95.559	105.033
Rub	6.446	6.500
Trim, Oil, Pack	27.272	22.175
Total	272.404	274.536

It is apparent that the difference between the two plants in man-hours required to produce this cabinet under comparable conditions was negligible.

As we have seen, the Adler Manufacturing Company cabinet was produced in 1941, while the figures on the cabinet at Mississippi Products, Inc., are those for 1950. During a nine-year period, in most lines of production, a decrease in man-hours per unit would be expected as the result of increased labor efficiency and the introduction of improved machines and production techniques, such as the Taylor Panel-Flo machine mentioned above. The total hours required by the Adler Company to produce 100 of these cabinets in 1941 was 324.959, while the time required at Mississippi Products, Inc., to produce a similar cabinet in 1950 was 302.805 hours. Converting these figures to output per man-hour, this represents an increase in productivity of 7.3 per cent in nine years.

IV

THE CASE OF "DAY-BRITE"

1. AVAILABILITY OF LABOR

The Labor Market. The town of Tupelo, the county seat of Lee
County, is located in the northeast portion of the State in what has
been in the past a predominantly agricultural area. The town has
shown considerable progress in the past few years, both in size and
in the occupational opportunities available to its citizens. From 1940
to 1950, the population rose from 8,212 to 11,527, an increase of 40
per cent. In the same period there was a small decrease in population
for Lee County and for the State of Mississippi.[1]

During the war and immediate postwar years, Tupelo made some
progress in its efforts to attract industrial establishments. In 1939,
there were 881 production workers employed in manufacturing establishments. By 1947, this number had increased to 1,485, an increase
of 68.5 per cent, as compared to an increase in Mississippi of 51.6 per
cent and in the United States of 52.6 per cent. At the same time, the
average size of manufacturing establishments increased more rapidly
in Tupelo than in either Mississippi or the United States. This was
borne out by the fact that the number of manufacturing firms in
Tupelo increased by only 24 per cent between 1939 and 1947, while
the increases for the United States and Mississippi were, respectively,
38.6 per cent and 60.5 per cent. In 1947, Tupelo had fifteen manufacturing plants employing twenty or more workers.[2]

In the period following World War II, business activity in general
in Tupelo was quite high.[3] Unemployment, even during the recon-
version period, presented no particular problem. The files of the local

[1]United States Bureau of the Census, "Mississippi, General Characteristics, 1950,"
Census of Population: 1950 (Washington: Government Printing Office, 1952),
Tables 25 and 43.

[2]United States Bureau of the Census, *Census of Manufactures, 1947,* (Washington: Government Printing Office, 1950), pp. 21, 332, and 333.

[3]"Index of business activity for the City of Tupelo," from the files of the Business Research Station, Mississippi State College.

Employment Security Commission office show that active applications on file for the three-county area of Itawamba, Lee, and Pontotoc Counties averaged about 1,100 with a range between 879 and 1,379 except during the 1946 rush of unemployment claimants under the G. I. Bill. According to those in charge of this office, ample labor was found to meet all demands during this period. The apparent contradiction of little unemployment and an adequate labor supply is to be explained by the fact that much of the growth in Tupelo's industrial labor force resulted from transfers from lower-paid occupations, especially in the rural areas nearby. It was estimated that 70 per cent of the industrial labor force in Tupelo lived outside the city, mostly on small farms.[4] Thus the tight housing situation that prevailed in Tupelo during this period was not a serious deterrent to the recruitment of industrial workers for plants in the city. Most of the workers continued to live on the farm and to commute daily by means, in most cases, of school buses, which were put to a double use, making four trips daily, two for industrial workers and two for school children. Many of these workers continued to operate agricultural enterprises, notably broiler production, in their spare time.[5]

The Employer. Such was the labor market when Day-Brite Lighting, Inc., of St. Louis decided to establish a subsidiary plant in Tupelo. Because of the influx of orders during the postwar period, the need for additional facilities became apparent and a survey of the possibilities of expanding the St. Louis plant did not appear particularly hopeful, either from the viewpoint of plant site or, more important, from that of meeting the increased personnel requirements. In addition, the capital requirements of such an addition would have placed the company in an awkward financial position. For all these reasons, it was decided that the additional factory space should be located outside the St. Louis area.

Several sites were investigated for adequacy of transportation, availability of raw materials, and existence of sufficient manpower. Tupelo met all these requirements, and in addition offered Day-Brite the opportunity to obtain use of a plant site and building to be built by the city of Tupelo and leased to the company at a nominal rent under

[4]Interview with Mr. L. T. McClellan, Manager, Tupelo Office, Mississippi Employment Security Commission.

[5]*Id.*

the Mississippi Balance Agriculture with Industry program. Further-
more, the company obtained remission of taxes for a period of five
years from the date of the beginning of construction of the plant.
These factors, together with the progressive appearance of the town,
seem to have been decisive in the final determination of the location
of the factory.

The Day-Brite Company manufactures fluorescent lighting fixtures,
according to copyrighted designs. The operation at Tupelo involves
all steps in this process, beginning with raw sheet steel and ending
with fixtures completed and packed for shipment to all parts of the
United States. The process includes the cutting, stamping, bending,
crimping, welding, and forming of metal parts which are assembled,
wired, and painted. It involves the use of heavy presses for the fabrication of parts to fairly close tolerance.

The parent company in St. Louis has for years bargained collective-
ly with a local union affiliated with the International Brotherhood of
Electrical Workers, AFL. A Tupelo local of this national union was
formed early in the history of the Tupelo plant and won recognition
in an NLRB representation election in April, 1948, only two or three
votes being cast against the union. The collective bargaining which
has been carried on since that time between the company and the
union has been harmonious. No work stoppages have occurred, and
neither party has charged the other with any unfair labor practice.
The 1952 contract between the company and the union differed from
the original contract mainly in revisions in wage rates and minor
changes in other various clauses. It contained a union shop clause,
under which all workers had to join the union after a probationary
period as a condition of continued employment. A seniority plan con-
trolled promotions and layoffs. Hospitalization and medical insurance
were financed jointly by the employer and the employees. A grievance
procedure provided for settlement of any dispute arising out of varying interpretations of the existing contract. Straight-time pay was
given for six holidays not worked, with the provision that any work
performed on those holidays would be paid for at double-time rates.

Preparation for operation of the plant was initiated by the management of the company when a plant manager and a maintenance
man with long experience with the company moved from the St. Louis
plant to Tupelo to supervise the installation of the machinery and
the commencement of the productive process. All other labor was

hired locally, including production workers of all ranges of skill, up to and including tool and die makers, clerical help, and supervisory employees. Starting in June, 1947, limited hiring of installation workers began. It was not, however, until February of 1948 that the hiring of operating personnel got under way. The labor force employed in this plant was not hired during a short hiring period, but rather grew to its size at the time of this study of 104 production workers over a period of years.

The local office of the Mississippi Employment Security Commission recommended 95 per cent of these workers to the company, the other 5 per cent being hired through personal acquaintances or through the recommendations of other employees. According to the manager of the plant, no difficulty was encountered in obtaining an adequate number of applicants for the jobs in the plants. As a matter of fact, the very large number of applicants in excess of those who might be considered for employment was a source of some embarrassment and after 1951 applications were discouraged because of the large number of applications on file.

The following table shows the number of production workers employed at this plant from its inception to March 1952.

Month	1947	1948	1949	1950	1951	1952
January		9	78	60	80	106
February		9	76	61	89	105
March		17	76	61	87	104
April		22	74	64	99	
May		27	49	64	103	
June		42	49	63	104	
July	1	51	49	66	103	
August	3	67	49	70	107	
September	3	80	59	74	107	
October	6	79	61	81	107	
November	9	79	61	82	107	
December	9	79	61	80	107	

The production workers when hired were all white males, a large per cent of whom were in their late twenties or early thirties. The policy of the company was to require a grammar school education for common labor and at least a partial high school education for machine operators. Colored men were used only in custodial capacities and were not considered among the production workers.

The original hiring rate established by the company for common labor was 60 cents per hour. This was increased to 70 cents when the first labor contract was signed with the union in April, 1948, and has been raised several times since then. The rate established in 1948 for machine helpers was 75 cents per hour and that for machine operators 95 cents per hour. For the more skilled jobs, rates were proportionately higher.

The Workers. After about four years of operation the management had succeeded in gathering together what it considered a dependable and efficient working force. As of the first of March, 1952, there were 104 production workers employed in the plant, ranging in age from seventeen to 52 years, with a median age of thirty years. The median years of school completed by these workers was ten and one-half. Of this group, 99 were married and five were single; 55 lived in Tupelo, 32 in Lee County, and seventeen in contiguous counties. No workers lived beyond counties contiguous to Lee County. All except three were born in the South, eleven being born in Tupelo, forty in Lee County, 32 in contiguous counties, seven elsewhere in Mississippi, and ten elsewhere in the South.[6] Nearly all of the employees lived in the immediate vicinity of Tupelo just prior to the acceptance of jobs at Day-Brite. There were 49 living in Tupelo, 26 in Lee County, fourteen in contiguous counties, none elsewhere in Mississippi, two elsewhere in the South, and one elsewhere in the United States. The labor market on which the establishment of this plant had impact was therefore strictly a local one.

These workers had varied major occupational experience: 24 in farming, sixteen in construction, 37 in manufacturing, six in transportation, ten in trade, seven in service industries, and one in government service. During the time of their major experience, 21 were unskilled workers, 46 semi-skilled, fourteen skilled, five clerical and sales, and five supervisory. From the above, it is apparent that a substantial fraction of the workers had their chief occupational experience in semi-skilled jobs in manufacturing plants.

The workers' experience in jobs held immediately prior to employment by Day-Brite Lighting, Inc., was as follows: fourteen came directly from farms, 22 from the construction industry, 33 from manu-

6The fact that some of these classifications do not total 104 is due to lack of information on some workers.

facturing, seven from transportation, fourteen from trade, one from finance, eight from service industries, and three from government service. It will be noted that ten fewer workers came directly from farms than the number for whom farming was the major experience. Also, more had construction as their latest experience, rather than as their major experience, probably as a result of the postwar building boom. Also of note is the larger number of cases where most recent experience was in trade than where major experience was in trade. This, and the situation in farming, mentioned above, may well have been due to the economic prosperity of the preceding few years and the accompanying increase in alternatives to farming as a means of gaining a livelihood.

There was an equal division between veterans and non-veterans: 51 veterans, and 51 non-veterans, and two whose status was unknown.

Among these workers, nineteen had had formal vocational training outside of the public schools as follows:

Auto mechanic	1
Woodwork and cabinet work	2
Construction	2
Business college	4
Electrical trades	3
Sheet metal and auto body	1
Welding and machine shop	3
Miscellaneous or mixed courses	1
Not elsewhere classified	2

2. TRAINABILITY

The Learning Period. It was impossible to make a learning curve for this group of workers. Lack of data on such jobs as might have lent themselves to such a process is partly responsible. The main difficulty, however, arose from the fact that those jobs for which data were available were by their very nature not suited to such investigation. The machine operators, for whom ample data were available, held complex jobs—jobs which because of the nature of the plant's operations were not confined to the tending of one machine. In order for the men to be effective, they had to be capable of operating a considerable number of different machines and of making the change from one to the other with a minimum disruption of the plant's schedule.

3. LABOR EFFICIENCY: MISSISSIPPI VERSUS NON-MISSISSIPPI

Absenteeism. The problem of absenteeism at this plant was so unimportant that no consolidated record of absenteeism was kept. From the very beginning of operations, the workers tended to show up on the job when scheduled to work. The following table, computed from a special analysis of payroll records, shows the average per cent of absenteeism of the workers for each year of the plant's operation.[7]

PERCENTAGE OF SCHEDULED DAYS ABSENT

1948	1.67
1949	1.83
1950	1.07
1951	1.59

Turnover. The labor turnover at this plant was small in comparison with that at plants doing similar work. The following table and graph show the comparative separation rates (exclusive of layoffs) at Day-Brite and at similar plants for the United States as a whole. The considerable drop in the rate at Day-Brite after the first few months of operation is typical of plants in the process of building up labor forces.

AVERAGE MONTHLY SEPARATION RATES EXCLUSIVE OF LAYOFFS AND MILITARY LEAVES AT DAY-BRITE LIGHTING, INC., AND SIMILAR INDUSTRY IN THE UNITED STATES

YEAR	DAY-BRITE	U. S.*
1948	2.4	3.9
1949	.9	1.7
1950	.9	2.4
1951	.6	3.0
1952**	.9	2.3

*Figures for 1948 and 1949 are those for the Stamped, Enameled, Galvanized Industries, while those for 1950 and later are for Metal Fabricating Industry. These figures are from the *Monthly Labor Review* published by the U. S. Department of Labor, Bureau of Labor Statistics.

**First two months of the year only.

Safety. Data were not obtainable on accident frequency and severity rates in this plant.

[7]See comparable data in absenteeism section of Chapter III.

Output. A comparison of the output per man-hour in the Tupelo plant with that of the St. Louis plant was confined to a relatively small number of items because of the necessity of comparing labor required to produce identical products by the use of similar methods. The two plants, to a very considerable extent, produced different products, and used different methods. Three identical items were found, however, produced in both plants by production methods also identical in certain stages of production. These three items were the electrical core, called the chassis, of a fluorescent lighting fixture (catalog No. 9987) and two items which were the outer portions into which the electrical core was fitted to produce a complete fixture (catalog Nos. 9996-W and 7792). The methods used in the fabricating process on these latter two fixtures were practically identical as far as concerned direct labor. The inclusion of indirect labor would have been detrimental to the showing of the St. Louis plant, since at that plant a wider variety of output necessitated a heavier employment of indirect labor. The following figures represent only direct labor.

The production of item No. 9987 was comparable in both plants in the fabrication department, where the metal was formed and assembled, and in the assembly-packing department, where the product was packed for shipment. In the fabrication department of Day-Brite, Tupelo, the number of hours of labor per 100 chassis produced was 8.11. At St. Louis, this operation required 8.30 hours per chassis. In the assembly-packing department, 8.29 hours were required at Tupelo to produce 100 items, while at the St. Louis plant the same number were produced in 7.2 hours. The wiring of 100 chassis required 10.32 hours at Tupelo and only 8.4 hours at St. Louis. There was, however, a difference in the production methods used in the wiring department. At Tupelo, prior to the wiring operation, a small eyelet was attached to each end of the wire; the 10.32 hours listed above included the time of the man operating the machine which attached these eyelets. In the St. Louis plant, no such device was used, the bare end of the wire being bent around the terminal before tightening. Both methods had been tried in both plants. In St. Louis the work of installing the wire went no faster when terminals were attached. In Tupelo, it was found that failure to have eyelets attached to the wire slowed the installation of the wiring considerably, and led to the conclusion that, to make the figures comparable, the time involved in attaching the eyelets should be included. The comparison of the time required to produce item No. 9987, insofar as fabrication and assembly packing were concerned (omitting the wiring operation), showed that the St. Louis plant required 5.49 per cent less labor per 100 items produced, or had a 5.81 per cent higher man-hour output. If the wiring operation were included, and if the time employed at Tupelo in attaching eyelets were also considered, the production of item No. 9987 was shown to have required 10.55 per cent less labor or that the plant in St. Louis had 11.8 per cent higher output per man-hour.

The production of item 9996-W involved no wiring. The time required in the prefabricating department to produce 100 of these enclosures was 18.27 man-hours at Tupelo, and 15.32 man-hours at St. Louis. The time required for assembly-packing of this item was 15.8 man-hours per 100 at Tupelo and 14.6 per 100 at St. Louis, representing a 12.18 per cent smaller labor requirement at the St. Louis plant and a 13.87 per cent greater output per man-hour. This part, together with the one discussed below, was spray-enameled and baked. The time required for this operation in the two plants could not be used for comparison because of irreconcilable differences in the techniques used.

For enclosure No. 7792, fabrication per 100 units required 12.31 man-hours in Tupelo and 12.9 in St. Louis. In the assembly-packing department, the time required at the Tupelo plant per 100 units of output was 17.4 hours, while that required at St. Louis was 15.6 hours. This indicated 4.07 per cent smaller number of hours required in the St. Louis plant or a 4.25 per cent greater output per man-hour.

When these rates of output were averaged for all three items, including the wiring operation on item 9987, the result showed that the output per man-hour in the St. Louis plant exceeded that of the Tupelo plant by about 10 per cent. Taking into consideration only the two departments where the operations were strictly comparable and excluding the wiring operation, which was of doubtful comparability, the average time for producing 100 of each of these items in the St. Louis plant was smaller by 7.8 per cent or that is to say, the output per man-hour in these operations averaged about 8.5 per cent higher in St. Louis than in the Tupelo plant.

V

THE CASE OF "PATHFINDER"

1. AVAILABILITY OF LABOR

The Labor Market. The Pathfinder Coach Division of Superior Coaches, Inc., was located in Kosciusko, Attala County, Mississippi, near the geographical center of the State. The territory surrounding Kosciusko is mostly sharply rolling hills, and the principal agricultural activity is logging, the county containing numerous sawmills, while dairying and the production of crops are relatively minor occupations. Only 23.2 per cent of the area in farms was in cropland as compared with 32.2 per cent for the State as a whole in 1949.[1]

In Kosciusko there was a milk canning plant, owned by one of the nationally known companies which furnished an outlet for milk which could not be sold in its fresh liquid form. Attala County was not one of Mississippi's wealthier counties. In 1939, its per capita income was $150 as compared with $201 for the State. In 1947, per capita income in Attala County had risen to $536 and that for the State to $663. The ratio of per capita income for Attala County to that for Mississippi increased from 74.6 per cent in 1939 to 80.8 per cent in 1947[2] shortly before the beginning of construction of the Pathfinder plant.

Over the past fifty years, the population of Attala County has been approximately stable and no great change has occurred in the racial

| | Kosciusko | Attala County | | |
Year	Total	White	Non-White	Total
1900	2,078	13,875	12,350	26,225
1910	2,385	15,624	13,227	28,851
1920	2,258	14,663	10,168	24,831
1930	3,237	15,157	10,878	26,035
1940	4,291	16,848	13,379	30,227
1950	6,758	15,084	11,568	26,652

[1]United States Bureau of Census, *U. S. Census of Agriculture, 1950* (Washington: Government Printing Office, 1952), Vol. I, Pt. 22, 20, 50.

[2]David McKinney, *Income Payments to Mississippians: County Estimates, 1939 and 1947* (University of Mississippi, Bureau of Business Research, 1952), p. 36.

composition of this population, as is indicated by the figures on page 43 taken from the censuses of population.

Kosciusko is the county seat of Attala County and the largest town in the county. As is the case in many other communities, a rather sharp increase in urban population has occurred, with Kosciusko growing rather rapidly, in contrast to the stability in population of the entire area. At the same time that the population was increasing, considerable manufacturing activity was developing in the town. In 1939 there were 32 manufacturing establishments and value added by manufacture was $1,400,000. The average number of employees was 1,014 in that year. By 1947 there were 33 manufacturing establishments and value added by manufacture was $6,400,000 per year. The average number of employees was 1,645 for that year. Ten of these establishments employed twenty or more workers, and these ten were engaged in businesses as follows: three in food and kindred products, one in textiles, five in the lumber industry, and one in chemicals. General business activity between 1940 and 1952 increased slightly less rapidly than did that for the State as a whole, as indicated by the following indexes:

INDEXES OF BUSINESS ACTIVITY FOR KOSCIUSKO AND MISSISSIPPI, 1940-1952*

	(1947-49 = 100)	
YEAR	KOSCIUSKO	MISSISSIPPI
1940	40.5	36.1
1941	41.1	44.5
1942	48.4	60.7
1943	52.7	70.0
1944	60.4	71.0
1945	67.1	72.0
1946	82.2	84.6
1947	92.1	92.8
1948	107.1	102.9
1949	100.1	104.4
1950	101.9	115.1
1951	118.1	122.9
1952	127.8	130.7

*The index for Kosciusko and vicinity was computed from data in the files of the Business Research Station of Mississippi State College, as was that for the State.

That the citizens of Kosciusko were convinced of the desirability of industrializing their community was indicated by the use they have made of the BAWI program. Under this program, the milk canning plant of the Pet Milk Company was brought to Kosciusko. The buildings of the Pathfinder Coach Division were constructed with an issue of $650,000 in bonds by the citizens of the community after an election in which the vote for the bond issue was 1,412 to 18. The Superior Coach Company put up over $1,000,000 for equipment and inventory.

Almost immediately after the bond election in mid-1950, construction was started on the plant. The employment of production workers began in early 1951, and the first completed bus was turned out in early May, 1951. When Superior Coaches, Inc., took over the buildings, six supervisory and administrative persons were sent to Kosciusko to commence operations. The rest of the workers at all skill levels, the office personnel, and the remaining administrative and executive officers were hired in the Kosciusko labor market. The company reported that ample applications for employment had been on file since the announcement that hiring would begin. As a matter of fact, one of the slightly embarrassing conditions which arose grew out of the inability of the company to give employment to all those who wished to be employed. This ample labor supply was available both during the time of plant construction and during the time when the plant was being manned with production workers. This was true despite the fact that, at those times, unemployment in the Kosciusko labor market was relatively low, having recovered after an increase due to the nation-wide recession in 1949. This is shown in the statistics concerning initial claims for unemployment compensation at the Kosciusko office of the Mississippi Employment Security Commission, which follow on page 46.

The Employer. The Pathfinder Coach Division of the Superior Coach Company of Lima, Ohio, was organized for the purpose of producing school bus bodies in the South in order to facilitate the delivery of the finished product to the Southern customer. Kosciusko was selected as a central point for delivery in the Southern and Southwestern states. In addition to school bus bodies, the parent company made ambulance and funeral coach bodies and street bus bodies for the Central and South American markets. Since the beginning of the operation of the Kosciusko plant, some ambulance and funeral

INITIAL CLAIMS, KOSCIUSKO LABOR MARKET
1948-1951

	1948	1949	1950	1951
January	134	262	384	270
February	251	714	275	168
March	66	125	129	72
April	51	473	148	194
May	90	495	130	67
June	67	120	125	64
July	71	518	121	386
August	43	189	79	66
September	20	111	49	74
October	17	135	60	82
November	29	154	135	182
December	62	284	136	

coach bodies have been produced here and the whole of the export operation of the parent company was, at the time of this study, located in Mississippi. The Pathfinder Coach Division was financed jointly by Attala County and the Superior Coach Company. The productive operation of the plant began in the second quarter of 1951 while construction was not yet completed. Training operations commenced at the fair grounds and continued there for several weeks before the building was sufficiently advanced to allow a shift to the permanent location.

With some 400 job openings available, the company solicited applications through one small ad in the local newspaper and a few spot announcements on the local radio. Approximately 5,000 applications for employment were taken in a very short time before a decision was made and announced to the public that no more applications would be received.

The entering rate for common labor, mostly Negroes, was 75 cents an hour, and that for most trainees, largely white people, 90 cents an hour. As of the date of this study, no general increases had been given, though a system of merit increases was in operation. W. W. McMillan, formerly the personnel manager of the plant, wrote: "We have found that here in the South as well as anywhere else the minimum rate will not hold a first-class worker; therefore, we have had to set up a plan for pretty rapid advancement up to the time the employee gets a decent living wage. At the present time our plant average hourly earnings is in the neighborhood of $1.50 and we ranked among the high paid industries in the State."[3]

In the period between March and November 1952 an incentive system was installed in all departments which, according to the company, was calculated to allow the workers to increase their earnings by approximately 25 per cent. In the plant, the men worked in pools, each of which had a leader, or working foreman, and the incentive plan was largely a pool incentive plan. Very few of the workers were on individual incentive.

A vacation plan, announced in the summer of 1952, allowed those workers with one year of service a one-week paid vacation. On November 1, 1951, an insurance plan was inaugurated providing for life insurance, weekly sick pay, and hospital and surgical benefits. On November 1, 1952, the benefits under this plan were considerably liberalized. No provision was made for paid holidays. In the summer of 1952, a federal credit union was organized, and it showed considerable growth in a very short period. The usual plant athletic teams were organized, but did not prove particularly successful in arousing employee enthusiasm, although the basketball teams played a schedule with out-of-town teams.

The rather loosely applied criteria by which the company selected its employees were as follows:

1. Preference was given to those under forty years of age with special effort to obtain employees between thirty and forty. The minimum age for males was eighteen years and that for females, nineteen years.

2. Preference was given to those workers with mechanical experience of one kind or another or with some evidence of mechanical aptitude.

3. For those employees who, it was hoped, might attain promotion, school attendance of at least eight years was required. No educational requirements were stressed in the case of ordinary production workers.

4. A good reputation as to general standing in the community and as to willingness to work was required in all cases.

The production of school bus bodies was found to be a rather highly seasonal operation. Most school authorities place orders for

[3]Letter to the authors from W. W. McMillan, Manager, Bus Sales, and former Personnel Manager, June 24, 1954.

buses during April and May, since it is at that time that school budgets are completed and plans are being made for the following year. Deliveries on these orders begin the early part of the summer and last until September, declining thereafter. The summer season was therefore the period of heavy employment at the Pathfinder Coach Division. With this situation in mind, the company instituted a policy of encouraging workers living on the farm to remain on the farm during their employment by the company. It was recognized that the seasonality in crop farming and that in the plant were not complementary but that, for many farming operations, the work demands of the company were fairly consistent with continued farming operations. In this plan, the company was fairly successful. Of the white males who were hired during the operation of the plant, 237 who lived previously in rural areas continued to live in rural areas. Only 26 who lived in rural areas moved to Kosciusko after being employed at Pathfinder Coach Division. Among colored males, seventeen who lived in rural areas continued to live there while only two moved from rural areas to Kosciusko.

Attempts on the part of two unions, the United Automobile Workers, CIO, and the Sheet Metal Workers, AFL, to organize the workers of the plant during the summer of 1952 were resisted by the company, but on petition of the workers the National Labor Relations Board ordered a representation election. By November 8, 1952, an indecisive election had been held in which neither a union nor "No union" received a majority. This necessitated a runoff election which was held subsequent to the cutoff date of this study. At the time of this writing the plant was still not organized.

The Workers. In this labor market the company was able to man its plant to its satisfaction. Employment of production workers from the beginning of hiring to November, 1952, had the sex-race distribution shown in Chart 6.

The vast majority of these workers were native to the area around Kosciusko, only three, or 1.0 per cent, being born outside the South, and only eighteen, or 6.0 per cent, outside Mississippi. Attala and contiguous counties accounted for 85 per cent. At the time of application for their employment, only one listed his address as outside the South, and only three, or 1.0 per cent, outside Mississippi. Residence in Attala or contiguous counties was shown by 95 per cent. The general characteristics of the various sex-race groups employed at the Pathfinder plant as of November 8, 1952, are revealed in the following tabulation:

CHARACTERISTICS OF PRESENT LABOR FORCE BY SEX AND RACE

	WHITE MALE	WHITE FEMALE	COLORED MALE
Median Age	31.2	34.5	32.3
Median Education	10.2	9.8	6.5
Marital Status:			
Single	8.0	. . .	16.3
Married	90.8	87.5	85.7
Divorced	1.2	12.5	. . .
Major Experience:			
Farming	42.6	. . .	52.8
Construction	11.0	. . .	12.8
Manufacturing	25.6	37.5	25.7
Trade	9.1	25.0	7.7
Service	5.5	37.5	. . .
Other	6.2	. . .	. . .
Major Skill Level:			
Unskilled	13.7	. . .	54.5
Semi-skilled	61.7	50.0	45.5
Skilled	12.5	25.0	. . .
Clerical and sales	6.9	12.5	. . .
Supervisory	5.4	12.5	. . .
Most Recent Job:			
Farm	26.7	. . .	35.2
Construction	17.5	. . .	18.9
Manufacturing	29.9	37.5	27.0
Trade	10.0	50.0	. . .
Service	7.2	12.5	13.5
Other	8.7	. . .	5.4
Most Recent Skill:			
Unskilled	21.6	. . .	68.2
Semi-skilled	53.0	37.5	31.8
Skilled	13.2	12.5	. . .
Clerical and sales	7.6	37.5	. . .
Supervisory	4.4	12.5	. . .

2. TRAINABILITY

The Training Program. Before the beginning of productive operations, a training program was employed consisting of instructions to the newly-hired workers by experienced employees brought to Kosciusko from the Lima plant of the parent company. At no time did

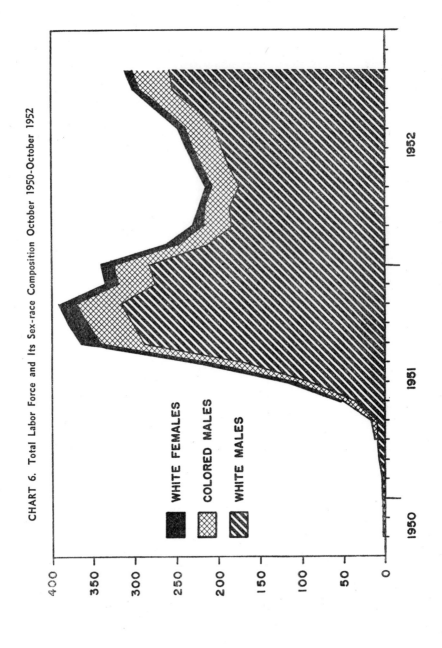

CHART 6. Total Labor Force and Its Sex-race Composition October 1950-October 1952

the number of instructors exceed nine (these were in addition to the six permanently transferred executives and supervisors).

After the plant began operation, the tasks were assigned to pools or groups, each of which had its own pool leader or working foreman. The incentive plan installed later provided for production bonuses to the workers which were dependent on the output of the pool, usually five or six workers. New, inexperienced workers were assigned to pools, and the pool leader and others in the pool were responsible for training them. Since the introduction of an inexperienced man into a pool would tend to reduce the output of the pool, lowering the production bonuses earned by its members, a plan was adopted whereby the time of the new man for the first two weeks was not charged against the pool. In exceptional cases this period was extended beyond two weeks.

Development of Productivity. No further information was available about the time required by employees of Pathfinder to become pro-ficient in the tasks to which they were assigned. There was available, however, information concerning the number of bus bodies produced each week between the week ending July 1, 1951, and the week ending September 7, 1952, and the number of man-hours required per unit during each of these weeks. There was a major defect in these data, since several different kinds of bus bodies were produced; and a mere statement of the number of units produced is not a complete description of the output for the week. This was considered to be a non-critical defect as there were no trends in the composition of the output from the early part of the period to later in the period, and therefore, the difference in composition between the output of one week and that of another was likely to show up as random variations in the data. The original data are shown in Chart 7, which indicates a close cor relation between the degree of utilization of the plant and the average number of man-hours per bus produced.[4]

In order to remove this factor and to clarify the effects of learning in the plant, a regression line was fitted to the data for output per week in buses and man-hours per bus in each week. The productivity attained during each succeeding week was then expressed as a percentage of the production which would have been expected during that week

4For detailed figures as furnished by the company, see Appendix C.

CHART 7.

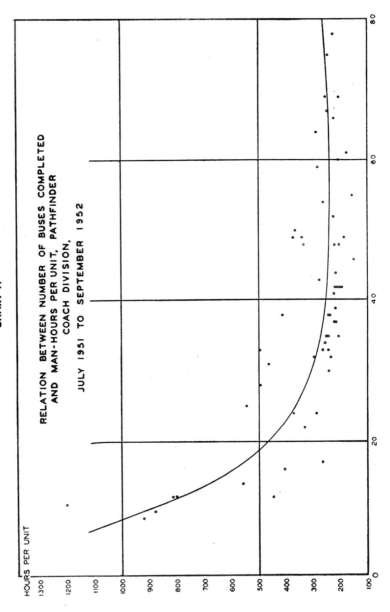

RELATION BETWEEN NUMBER OF BUSES COMPLETED
AND MAN-HOURS PER UNIT, PATHFINDER
COACH DIVISION.
JULY 1951 TO SEPTEMBER 1952

in view of the degree of plant utilization as shown on the regression line. The results are shown in Chart 8.

Two trends are easily discernible. Between the first of July and the latter part of August, 1951, there was a marked decline in productivity. This might be accounted for by either or both of two conditions: (1) the early high productivity may have been a result of the enthusiasm of the workers in the operation of the new plant, or (2) the

CHART 8. Adjusted Hours as Per Cent of Actual Hours, Pathfinder July 1951 to September 1952

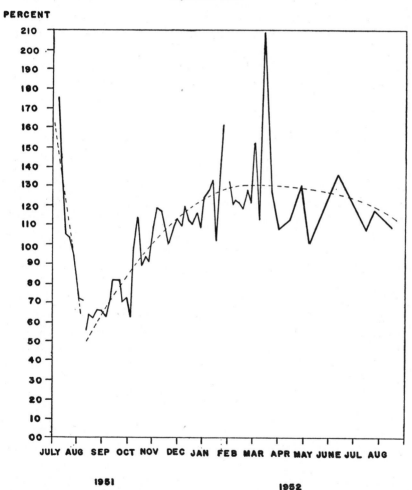

early buses produced in the new plant were in part merely assembled
from parts fabricated in the parent plant in Lima, Ohio.

The next trend discernible, the early part of which was obscured by
the trend noted above, was a growth in productivity lasting from the
beginning of production, perhaps, until April, 1952, a period of about
ten months. From July to November, 1951, new persons were being
added to the payroll; from November, 1951, until April, 1952, the
number of workers was decreasing. This ten-month period did not
represent the length of time required for a worker to learn his job,
since new and untrained individuals were being added constantly.
From April, 1952, to September, 1952, the trend was apparently downward. This was the period during which employment was being increased from its low point in April and the reduction in productivity
was probably the result of the introduction of untrained workers who
had not as yet had sufficient experience to gain maximum efficiency.

3. LABOR EFFICIENCY:
MISSISSIPPI VERSUS NON-MISSISSIPPI

Absenteeism. Two distinct influences seem to have been present in
the absentee experience, shown in Chart 9. First, during the first six
weeks of the company's operation after July 1, 1952, the rate of absenteeism rose very rapidly, probably as a result of the scheduling of
operations on a ten-hour day and six-day week (in some departments
on a twelve-hour day) in an effort to catch up with the backlog of
orders which had grown up during the delay in the commencement
of production. Second, in August, the working schedule was reduced,
and the absentee rate declined precipitously. After this time, the trend
in the absentee rate seems to be best described by a segment of a
second-degree parabola which reached its minimum point in June
and July of 1952 and increased slightly thereafter. June and July of
1952 represented the period of expanding employment in the company's seasonal operation. It would appear that the normal tendency,
inasfar as it was revealed during this short period, was for the absentee
rate to decline as workers gained experience. The slight upturn in the
absentee rate after July, 1952, may have been due to the introduction
of inexperienced workers during the process of increasing the labor
force. In the case of this plant, as in other cases, no comparable data
for non-Southern plants or for the nation as a whole were available

CHART 9. Hours Absent as Per Cent of Hours Scheduled, Pathfinder June 1951 to November 1952

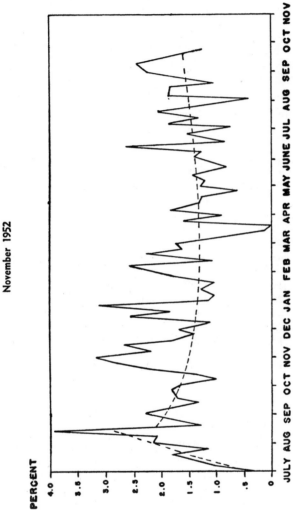

for comparison with the experience of the Pathfinder Coach Division other than the 1947 data in Chapter III, page 24.

Turnover. The employment of production workers and the orderly production of buses began in June, 1951. The following table shows the monthly separation rate from that date to the end of October, 1952, and a comparison with the same rate for the whole automobile transportation equipment industry. (Layoffs were excluded from both of these series.) It will be noted that the average monthly separation rate during this period for the Pathfinder Coach Division (2.41) was materially below the average monthly rate during the same period for the transportation equipment, automobile, industry as a whole (2.88).

SEPARATION RATE (EXCLUDING LAYOFFS AND MILITARY
SEPARATIONS) PATHFINDER COACH DIVISION
AND EQUIPMENT, AUTOMOBILE, FOR
UNITED STATES

	1951			1952	
MONTH	UNITED STATES	PATHFINDER	MONTH	UNITED STATES	PATHFINDER
June	3.2	1.29	Jan.	1.5	4.35
July	2.3	3.22	Feb.	.4	3.30
Aug.	2.4	5.41	Mar.	1.4	.90
Sept.	2.1	5.00	Apr.	1.8	2.76
Oct.	1.9	2.92	May	1.7	0
Nov.	1.3	.84	June	1.9	.43
Dec.	1.0	.60	July	1.6	2.07
			Aug.	2.3	3.50
			Sept.	3.4	2.44
			Oct.	3.4	1.95

This same information is shown graphically in Chart 10. Note that the high points in the separation rate at the Pathfinder Coach Division do not coincide, to any noticeable extent, with periods of maximum demand for agricultural labor. In other words, there is no indication that this separation rate can be explained in important part by the periodic shifting of laborers to farm work during peak planting or harvesting seasons.

On the basis of the limited period covered by the data, it would appear that the overall trend in the separation rate, exclusive of layoffs, for the Pathfinder Coach Division was slightly downward throughout the period under consideration.

Safety. Accident frequency and severity rates in the Pathfinder Coach Division were high during the first few months of operation but declined rapidly thereafter. The following table shows the ac-

CHART 10. Separations Excluding Layoffs, Pathfinder Coach Division and U. S. Auto Transportation Equipment Industry, June 1951 to October 1952

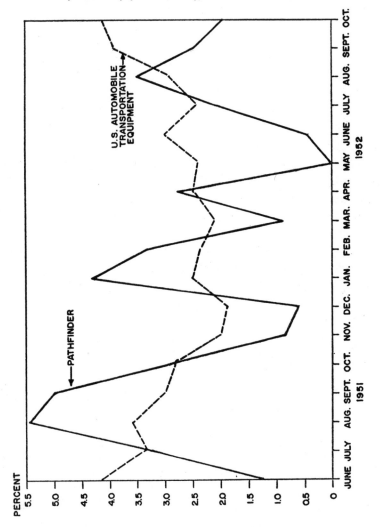

cident frequency rate for the five quarters for which the plant had
been in operation, together with comparable data for the United
States as a whole.

ACCIDENT FREQUENCY RATES

PERIOD	PATHFINDER COACH DIVISION	TRANSPORTATION EQUIPMENT MOTOR VEHICLES, BODIES AND TRAILERS, UNITED STATES*
1951		
3rd Quarter	49.2	6.5
4th Quarter	49.8	6.0
1952		
1st. Quarter	18.1	5.5
2nd. Quarter	10.8	5.4
3rd. Quarter	21.5	4.6

*U. S. Bureau of Labor Statistics, *Monthly Labor Review*, Preliminary Injury
Reports; Chart 11 illustrates this same information.

Notice that even the marked reduction in accident frequency after
the second quarter of operation still left the rate at the Pathfinder
Coach Division above the average for the industry in the United
States. The upturn in accident frequency in the third quarter of 1952
coincided with the rather heavy increase in employment during that
quarter and may have resulted from the introduction of a considerable number of inexperienced workers.

The severity rate in this plant is shown in the following figures:

PERIOD	SEVERITY RATE
1951	
3rd. Quarter	12.77
4th. Quarter	.05
1952	
1st. Quarter	.07
2nd. Quarter	.02
3rd. Quarter	.22

A large portion of the high severity rate in the third quarter of 1951
is attributable to a single major accident which occurred during that
time when few production workers were employed. The only data
available for comparison is an annual severity rate in the transporta-

tion equipment industry for the United States for the year 1951, which
rate was 0.7. This rate exceeded that at the Pathfinder Coach Division
in all periods except the third quarter of 1951.

Output. A comparison of the output of the Pathfinder Coach Division with that of the Lima, Ohio, plant of the parent company can

CHART 11. Accident Frequency Rates, Pathfinder Coach Division and U. S. Average for
Transportation Equipment, Motor Vehicles, Bodies and Trailers,
3rd Quarter 1951 to 4th Quarter 1952

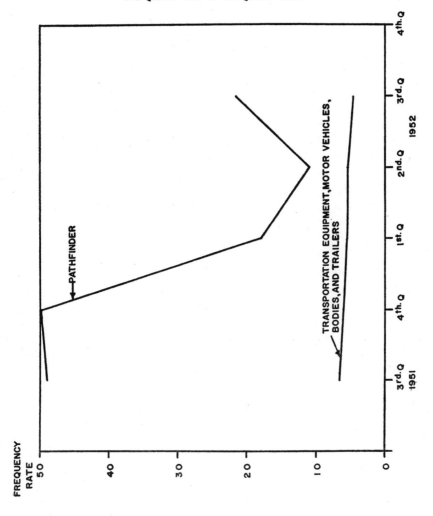

be made in connection with the production of a "standard" 21' 8"
bus body. The Lima plant had not produced this body for two years,
but when such production was under way, the methods and equipment used were the same as those used in the Kosciusko plant inasfar
as most of the departments were concerned. One department, where
the methods differed, was omitted, as was one where data on the experience at Kosciusko were not in such form as to be comparable.

Leaving out the non-comparable departments, the amount of direct
labor required to produce the "standard" body at the Lima, Ohio,
plant was 67.0 hours, while the same operations in the production of
the same unit at the Kosciusko plant required 64.0 hours of direct
labor. This indicates that approximately 4.5 per cent fewer hours
were required at the Kosciusko plant than in the non-Mississippi
plant, or that output per hour was 4.7 per cent higher in the Mississippi plant.

In addition to this comparison of overall productivity there were
available data on the comparative output of single departments which
were of interest because of the sex-race composition of the workers. In
the paint departments, where Negroes were used exclusively at Kosciusko and white men at Lima, the amount of time spent on each
"standard" body was 5.9 hours at Lima and 7.0 hours at Kosciusko.
This indicates that approximately 16 per cent less time was consumed
by workers in the Lima plant for this operation.

One department which was omitted from the consideration above
was the Trim Shop, where the seats are produced and upholstered. In
Kosciusko this work was done mainly by white women while in Lima
it was done by white men. As of the periods compared above, the
methods used in the two plants differed, the workers at Lima "spitting
tacks" while those at Kosciusko used stapling machines. Since that
time the new method had been adopted in the Northern plant, and,
as of the date of this study, the two operations were strictly comparable. To construct and upholster the seats of the "standard" bus
referred to above required 1.27 hours of direct labor at Lima and 1.37
man-hours at Kosciusko, or about 7 per cent more man-hours at the
Pathfinder Plant than in the plant of the parent company.

VI

ARE ALL MISSISSIPPI WORKERS ADAPTABLE TO INDUSTRIAL WORK?

1. INTRODUCTION

So FAR WE HAVE been comparing the performance of Mississippi workers with that of workers in non-Mississippi plants and in the nation as a whole. The question might arise, "Are these a selected group of Mississippians or do they represent Mississippi labor in general?" That is to say, can we find represented here any important segment of the population of Mississippi which is particularly adaptable or unadaptable to industrial employment? On the answer to this question depends the size of the potential. If there are certain groups in the State who are unfit or unadaptable to industrial employment, then the degree to which Mississippi can be industrialized will be reduced in proportion to the number of these groups represented in the total population.

For instance, the Mississippi population is made up of two sexes and, in the main, two races, white and colored males and white and colored females. If even one of these sex-race groups is found to be deficient in its ability to adapt to an industrial environment, then the industrial potential of Mississippi is considerably less than it would otherwise be. Since we cannot meaningfully compare these sex-race groups with like sex-race groups outside the State, it is necessary to depend in our reasoning on the following kind of organization. In the first part of this study, we have compared the working forces of these plants with those of other plants or of the nation as a whole to discover the success of the total force in industrial employment. On the whole, Mississippi labor has not shown up badly in this comparison. The performance of any component of Mississippi labor forces can be ascertained by a comparison with the performance for the whole group: i.e., if it were found that the average turnover rate for Mississippi workers compared favorably with that of workers in other areas, a finding that one segment of these labor forces had a materially lower turnover rate than the rest would indicate that this segment of the labor force compared better than favorably in this connection with the workers of the nation as a whole. A failure to find any group with a turnover rate materially higher than the average for the group as a whole indicates that insofar as these labor forces represent a cross-section of Mississippi population, all segments of the Mississippi population perform satisfactorily with regard to turnover.

One of the purposes of this study was to get information about the potential labor force of the State available for new industrial plants. This was a very difficult task: it was impossible to identify the individuals making up this universe inasmuch as there is no way of telling what individuals in some future Mississippi population might be willing to transfer from whatever they were doing at the time to employment in the new plant at the wages offered and under the working conditions furnished by the plant and who would have the skills, as yet unknown, and other characteristics to meet the requirements of their possible future employers.

Only one thing is known for sure about this potential labor force. The workers in these three plants were, a short time before the study was made, members of the potential labor force of Mississippi. In reading the conclusion that follows, it should be kept in mind that any generalizations are of limited applicability. In the first place, these conclusions should be applied only with caution to workers in plants which differ materially in product, process, or managerial techniques from the three plants studied. At the time this study was made, the labor market from which the workers were drawn was relatively tight when compared with the market at any time except the war period. In a time of relatively high unemployment, these conclusions might not hold, in that management's freedom of choice would be greater and in that the resulting labor force might have characteristics more desirable than those found in this study.

In ascertaining the adaptability of the characteristic groups, only partial success was achieved, since many degrees of the chosen characteristics were not represented in the payrolls of the three plants, and, therefore, fell outside these generalizations. For instance, the number of white women employed as production workers was so small that only the most general statements could be made about them. In none of these plants were Negro women employed as production workers. Again, only the age group from about twenty to about forty was well represented among the workers on whom data were gathered.

To each of the major groups of this population, then, were applied such measures of performance as the data justified.[1] There were five of these measures which were meaningful and for the computation of which data were available:

1. *Absence Rate.* These data concerned absences which were beyond the control of the employer, and, therefore, excluded leaves of absence. No attempt was made to differentiate between excused and unexcused absences, illness and non-illness absences, etc., since there was some doubt as to the accuracy of such differentiation in the records, and since the effect on productivity of a lost day's work is independent of the reason for it. Two measures were used to express absence rates: (1) in two plants, the average number of regularly scheduled days per year on which the worker did not report for work, and (2) in one plant, the per cent of regularly scheduled work days during which the worker was absent. One of these measures could have been transposed into the other, but this was avoided—in part, to emphasize the unsuitability of all of these measures for making comparisons between plants. It is only where one group within a plant is compared with another group within that plant that meaningful conclusions can be drawn. To go beyond this might lead to invalid conclusions, since the different environments in which these people worked in the three plants may have led to variations in absence rates that were not related to the topic under consideration.

2. *Turnover.* Rate of turnover was measured by computing the separation rate (excluding layoffs, leaves of absence, and military leave) in much the same way that the separation rates mentioned earlier in this work were computed. Since we could not get the total number of persons on the payroll during the week containing the middle of the month, average employment was the average of that on the first of the month and at the end of the month.

3. *Output.* The explanation of the degree of success attained by these characteristic groups in output per man-hour presented difficulties which limited possible generalizations. Data that would reflect the ability and willingness of the worker to produce required certain

[1]These data did not permit the drawing of conclusions, within measurable limits of error, about the relative performances of characteristic groups in other populations than the plants studied. They should be interpreted according to the reader's own judgment of the importance of the relative difference in performance under the conditions described.

characteristics in the nature of the job to be studied: (1) there had
to be records of the output of each individual worker. This ruled out
jobs normally falling under group incentive plans and those on time
rate payments with no production records. (2) The rate of output
had to be under the control of the individual worker and not dependent upon the speed of other workers or the rate of operation of
a machine or conveyor belt. (3) In addition, the job classifications had
to cover enough employees to permit the drawing of dependable
conclusions.

At Mississippi Products, Inc., seven job classifications in three different departments were considered suitable by these criteria. Five of
these classifications were drawn from the Finish Mill. These were:
(1) Variety Sawyer, (2) Boring Machine Operator, (3) Hand Shaper
Operator, (4) Router Operator, and (5) Double-End Tenoner Operator. From the Cabinet Assembly Department the classification of
Hand Block Sander was chosen, and from the Rub Department, the
classification, Rubber. This selection of classifications had certain
unavoidable disadvantages. In the first place, no women could be
included in this portion of the study, as women did not hold these
jobs. Further, a difficulty arose in measuring the comparative productivity of white males and colored males, since in only one of these
classifications, i.e. Hand Block Sanding, were both to be found, and
it was predominantly manned by colored men, with only a few white
men for comparison.

The method used for analyzing output of various characteristic
groups was as follows: for each classification, records of individual
output were obtained for a period of three weeks during February,
1951. This period was chosen because of the stable level of operation
and because few new employees were hired during the period.

Mississippi Products, Inc., operated in these classifications on an
incentive based on a normal hour's output. When a worker produced
during an eight-hour day more than eight times this standard hour's
work, he was said to have "earned" more than eight hours and was
paid accordingly. If a worker "earned" more than eight hours during
an eight-hour day he received a bonus at the end of the week for that
excess output regardless of his output during the remainder of the
week. The records then showed hours worked and earned hours, and
earned hours were proportional to physical output.

Hours worked and hours earned were used to compute the fraction of standard which each employee averaged each week. Then for each week a weighted average of the performance of the group in the classification was computed, and the performance of each individual was expressed as a percentage of the average performance of the group. The output records shown below for various characteristic groups are made up of the median per cent of average per cent of standard of the employees composing the characteristic group.

Conditions in the Day-Brite Lighting, Inc., plant limited considerably the value of the intra-plant comparisons of productivity. The data available on output were limited, since the plant did not operate under the incentive plan and records of individual production were kept only for operators of presses in the fabrication department. Data on the output of these men could easily be collected and assigned to individuals, inasmuch as the machines being operated were equipped with counters, while other operations in the plant were such that the determination of individual output would require considerable effort and expense.

Because of the varied nature of the tasks performed by these press operators, it was necessary to include the records of production over a relatively long period of time. Records for 1949 were considered, and only those operators working in one of the measured jobs of substantial portion of that year were included in the following comparisons. These limitations so reduced the number of cases available as to make comparison profitable only where dichotomies could be established.

Since none of the jobs at the Pathfinder plant met the requirements necessary to allow comparisons of average outputs of persons falling within various groups, the output measures could not be made for these workers.

4. *Promotional Progress.* The relative success of the different characteristic groups in increased efficiency during the time of employment could be measured by comparing the amount of time spent at one skill level before promotion to a higher skill level. Rapid promotion may mean either one of two things. It may mean that a person with considerable skill acquired from previous experience was able to convince his superior that he deserved such promotion. Or it may mean that an untrained person showed particular aptitude in training and was ready, after a short period, for promotion.

Promotion to a higher skill level is not solely a measure of ability to hold a higher skilled job. It depends in part on opportunity. The speed of promotional progress means only that management, as better jobs become available, selected certain persons for promotion for some reason, be it efficiency, attitude, or any other characteristic which management considered desirable in employees.

The job evaluation plan at Mississippi Products, Inc., divided all job classifications into seven skill levels ranging from unskilled to most skilled. Skill level 6 was commonly employed as the entering classification for trainee machine operators. Upon the completion of training the worker was promoted to skill level 5. Skill level 4 was attained when the operator became sufficiently expert to do all set-ups on the less complicated machines. Skill level 3 was reserved for operators with the ability to do all set-ups on the more complicated machines. Skill levels 2 and 1 were not open to machine operators, but were reserved for maintenance men and craftsmen.

There were no white people in skill level 7. There were few Negroes above skill level 6, and none above skill level 4. Certain jobs were manned by white men, certain jobs by white women, and certain jobs by colored men, and some jobs were occupied by two or all of these groups. So few white women and colored males were promoted between skill levels 6 and 5 and skill levels 5 and 4 that analysis was not considered profitable. The few who were promoted could not be considered in combination with the white men promoted inasmuch as the sex-race groups were non-competing and any differences in the time required to attain promotion could not be attributed to differences in trainability as they might result from management preferences between the sex-race groups.

The Mississippi Products, Inc., analysis was based on promotions of white males during 1950 and the first seven or eight months of 1951. It excluded promotions covering two or more skill levels at one jump. The necessity of accepting these limitations reduced the number of cases for analysis to such an extent that only the group promoted from skill level 6 to skill level 5 and the group promoted from 5 to 4 contained enough cases to provide meaningful conclusions. And even in these groups, the amount of detail breakdown had to be limited. The analysis covered sixty cases of promotion from skill level 6 to skill level 5 and fifty cases from skill level 5 to skill level 4.[2]

At Day-Brite Lighting, Inc., only one promotion, that of machine operator helper to machine operator, had occurred a sufficient number of times to warrant even the simplest analysis. Even here the small number of cases necessitated the use of dichotomic analysis.

In the case of Pathfinder Coach Division three instances were found where promotions from one skill level to another had been numerous enough to allow a meaningful breakdown into characteristic groups. These were the promotion of colored males from skill level 1 to skill level 2; the promotion of white men from skill level 3 (primarily a training classification) to skill level 5 (primarily a semi-skilled operator classification); and the promotion of white males from skill level 5 to skill level 6 (the lower of the two skill levels made up of skilled jobs.)[2]

5. *Layoff Rate.* Using the same technique as was employed with the separation rate, it was possible to compute another rate with considerably different significance. This was called the layoff rate, and in plants where management's evaluation of the worker played a major part in the selection of those individuals who were to be laid off, it gave an objective measure of management opinion of the various groups constituting the labor force. These differences in layoff rates may have been the result of conscious policy determinations or of an evaluation of each individual worker. The actual size of the figures on layoff rates had no meaning for our purpose, since they were chiefly a function of the market for the employer's product.

Note that the first three of these performance measures are fairly objective, while the last two reflect, to a considerable extent, managements' opinions of the performances of employees, as shown by managerial actions on occasions when selective judgment was necessary.

2. SEX-RACE GROUPS

Since colored males represent a large proportion of the Mississippi population and since their employment in industry is fairly limited and fairly late, any measures of their adaptability as industrial employees is of importance. The same is true of the measures of performance of another considerable fraction of the population, white females. On the other hand, though white males have been employed considerably as industrial workers, measures of their performance are

[2]Note that the skill level numbering systems were in opposite directions in the Mississippi Products and Pathfinder plants. (See Appendices A and C.)

inadequate and undependable, so that any more exact information on their experience would also be worth while. An investigation into the ability of colored females as production workers was made impossible by the fact that none of these three plants employed them as such. It should be noted that the information on men of both races was based on much more adequate data than the conclusions with regard to white women, few of whom were employed in these plants.

The following table shows the absence records of these sex-race groups in the two plants in which records that could be used for this purpose were available.

ABSENCE RATES

SEX-RACE GROUP	MISSISSIPPI PRODUCTS, INC. (Median days absent per year)	PATHFINDER (Per cent of total scheduled hours absent)
White males	4.00	1.10
White females	4.33	.95
Colored males	3.00	.50

(No attempt should be made to draw comparisons between plants since the data are not comparable.) Note that the absentee records of colored males were substantially better than those of white males and of white females in the two plants. On the other hand, white females' absentee rates varied little from those of white males, being slightly higher in one plant and slightly lower in the other.

The following table shows average monthly separation rates excluding layoffs and military leaves. This table shows that colored males had substantially lower rates in both plants than did white males. White females in one plant had a slightly lower separation rate than did white males. In the other plant which used white females,

SEPARATION RATES

SEX-RACE GROUP	MISSISSIPPI PRODUCTS, INC.	PATHFINDER
White males	1.8	10.6
White females	1.4	6.0
Colored males	.9	6.3

they had a separation rate lower than that for either of the male categories.

Records of output per man-hour were not available for white females, and were available for only a relatively small number of white males and colored males. Of particular difficulty was the comparison between the output per man-hour for white and colored males, inasmuch as employment of the two groups in the same job was uncommon. The rather meager indication obtained from data on a small number of workers in one of the plants disclosed no difference in output per man-hour for these two groups.

The rates of promotional progress and the layoff rates for the different sex-race groups were not considered comparable because of the considerable possibility that company policy, personal preference of superiors, and the general social atmosphere would have more to do with the size of these rates than would the nature of the individual's record.

3. AGE GROUPS

Given the degree of success in output of Mississippi workers in general, a question remains as to whether or not those of the various age groups are equally adaptable to industrial employment. Can, for instance, the older workers, most of whose lives have been spent in a little-mechanized Mississippi, adjust themselves to the highly-mechanized industrial environment? Or, on the other hand, do young Mississippians, who constitute a larger proportion of the population in this State than in most others,[3] make good industrial workers?

The information available in this matter was of limited use since the vast majority of the workers fell between the ages of twenty and forty. Any generalizations drawn then would have only strictly limited applicability to workers of 45 and none whatever to persons of 65.

The following table shows the absence rates for the various age groups in the plants studied. So few white females were employed in any of the plants that they were not included in the table. In all three plants, workers in the older age groups, both white and colored males, tended to be absent less than those in the younger age groups, with the possible exception of those over 55 years of age, for whom the data were so limited as to be useless.

3See Appendix F.

ABSENCE RATES

AGE GROUP	MISSISSIPPI PRODUCTS (MEDIAN DAYS ABSENT PER YEAR)		DAY-BRITE (MEDIAN DAYS ABSENT PER YEAR)	PATHFINDER (PER CENT OF SCHEDULED HOURS ABSENT)	
	White Males	Colored Males	White Males	White Males	Colored Males
15 and under 20	..	..	5.2	1.2	2.9
20 and under 25	4.3	3.7	3.4	1.6	1.3
25 and under 30	4.3	3.5	2.0	1.4	.8
30 and under 35	4.1	3.7	2.4	1.6	.4
35 and under 40	4.0	2.9	1.9	.9	.2
40 and under 45	3.7	2.2	1.8	.6	.3
45 and under 50	3.7	2.7	2.2	.5	.1
50 and under 55	3.7*	.8	3.3*	.0	.0
55 and under 60	..		..	1.4*	2.1*

*Less than three cases

The table on page 72 shows separation rates excluding layoffs by age group. Except in the case of colored males in one plant, the separation rate (excluding layoffs) for the older workers was materially less than that for the younger workers.

Information concerning individual output made it possible to compare the performance of the various characteristic groups in only two of the plants. Even here the number of cases concerned was smaller than would have been desirable.

The following table shows the output of the age groups. The figures for Day-Brite Lighting, Inc., apply to white males only, but those for Mississippi Products, Inc., include the records of a limited number of colored males.

OUTPUT

Age Group	Mississippi Products*	Day-Brite*
20 and under 25	103.4	90.8
25 and under 30	94.3	90.8
30 and under 35	95.4	
35 and under 40	98.0	101.8
40 and over	104.3	

*See description of units, pp. 64 and 65.

At Mississippi Products, Inc., a considerable advantage in productivity lay with the twenty and under 25 age group and the forty and over age group. In the case of Day-Brite Lighting, Inc., those of age thirty and above had a considerably better record than those below thirty.

It was possible to get comparisons between the time required for different age groups to obtain promotion in two cases for Mississippi Products, Inc., in one for Day-Brite Lighting, Inc., and in three for Pathfinder, including one for colored males. There seems to have been no consistent relationship between age and speed of promotion. The older and younger groups made the semi-skilled promotion at about the same rates of speed, and though the younger group were promoted to skilled work more rapidly in one plant, the older group were promoted more rapidly in the other plant in which skilled promotions were studied.

Layoff rates were considered meaningful at only two of the plants studied, since at the third plant seniority played a major part in de-

SEPARATION RATES

AGE GROUP	Mississippi Products		Day-Brite	Pathfinder	
	White Males	Colored Males	White Males	White Males	Colored Males
Under 24	15.4	9.6			
24 and under 30 ...	10.4	6.5	1.4	2.8	1.4
30 and under 36 ...	6.8	5.5			
36 and over	5.7	4.2	.7	1.4	1.4

PROMOTION RATES

AGE GROUPS	Mississippi Products		Day-Brite		Pathfinder	
	Skill Level 6 to 5 WHITE MALES	Skill Level 5 to 4 WHITE MALES	Helper to Operator WHITE MALES	Skill Level 1 to 2 COLORED MALES	Skill Level 3 to 5 WHITE MALES	Skill Level 5 to 6 WHITE MALES
	(Months)	(Months)	(Days)	(Days)	(Days)	(Days)
Under 30	4.0	4.0	63	60	41	200
30 and over ...	4.0	7.0	65	45	43	95

termining who should be laid off when business became slack and
this situation removed to a certain extent management's function of
selecting those to be laid off. The following table shows the layoff
rates for the various age groups in the two plants. From these data
it is quite apparent that management, after trying them for a time,
preferred the older workers to the younger workers.

LAYOFF RATES

	MISSISSIPPI PRODUCTS		PATHFINDER	
AGE GROUPS	White Males	Colored Males	White Males	Colored Males
Under 24	1.2	1.3	3.6	5.1
24 and under 30	.8	1.2		
30 and under 36	.6	1.1	2.1	3.0
36 and over	.7	.9		

4. EDUCATION GROUPS

There are in Mississippi many white people and even more Negroes[4]
with no great number of years of formal education. If Mississippi is to
become highly industrialized, many of these people with little formal
education must be employed in industry. The question then arises,
"Are there differences between the industrial performances of the
various education-level groups?"

The following table shows the relation between education and absence rates.

ABSENCE RATES

	MISSISSIPPI PRODUCTS		DAY-BRITE	PATHFINDER (PER CENT OF TOTAL SCHEDULED HOURS ABSENT)	
	(MEDIAN DAYS ABSENT PER YEAR)		(MEDIAN DAYS ABSENT PER YEAR)		
EDUCATION GROUPS	White Males	Colored Males	White Males	White Males	Colored Males
Under 5	4.4	3.1	9.7*	.1	.6
5 and under 9	4.4	3.2	2.4	1.0	.4
9 and under 13	4.2	3.3	2.6	1.2	.6
13 and under 17 ...	2.0	..	..	2.0	..

*Less than three cases

[4]See Appendix F.

Workers with more education tended to be absent more than those with less education; for white males in one plant, absenteeism was higher among those with less education, while in all other cases where a trend was discernable, the opposite was true.

The following table shows the relations between education levels and average monthly separation rates excluding layoffs. This evidence is almost completely inconclusive: in the three cases where white males were considered, slightly lower separation rates were computed for those with more education, while in the third case, the opposite was true; in the two computations for colored males, the results differed in direction.

SEPARATION RATES

| EDUCATION GROUPS | MISSISSIPPI PRODUCTS | | DAY-BRITE | PATHFINDER | |
	White Males	Colored Males	White Males	White Males	Colored Males
Under 10	10.5	6.2	1.0	2.1	..
10 and over	9.6	8.8	1.1	1.8	..
Under 6	..	5.6	..	..	1.6
6 and over	...	7.7	..	..	1.4

The effect of education on the output of employees is given in the following table showing median per cents of average output for the various education groups. At Mississippi Products, Inc., those with more education had a slight advantage in productivity. At Day-Brite Lighting, Inc., however, the reverse was indicated.

OUTPUT

| EDUCATION GROUPS | MISSISSIPPI PRODUCTS | | | DAY-BRITE |
	Finish Mill	Hand Block Sanders	Rubbers	Press Operator
Under 5	62.1*	..	100.9	⎫ 100.6
5 and under 9	91.3	92.4	100.1	
9 and under 13	99.2	112.2	105.3	
13 and over	78.0*	..	112.9*	⎬ 97.1

*Less than three cases.

In the following table, the relation between the level of education and the cases of promotion meeting the criteria already outlined is set forth. For the lower skilled jobs, those white males with less education attained promotion in a somewhat shorter time. In the somewhat higher skilled jobs, the evidence is contradictory. For colored males, the higher education group was promoted in a considerably shorter length of time.

PROMOTION RATES

	MISSISSIPPI PRODUCTS		DAY-BRITE	PATHFINDER		
	Skill Level 6 to 5	Skill Level 5 to 4	Helper to Operator	Skill Level 1 to 2	Skill Level 3 to 5	Skill Level 5 to 6
EDUCATION GROUPS	WHITE MALES (Months)	WHITE MALES (Months)	WHITE MALES (Days)	COLORED MALES (Days)	WHITE MALES (Days)	WHITE MALES (Days)
Under 10	3	5	55	..	41	86
10 and over	4	3	84	..	43	150
Under 7	..	..	..	60	..	..
7 and over	..	..	..	30	..	..

Management's preference for workers of various educational attainments, after such persons had been employed for a certain period of time, is shown in the following table of layoff rates for the various education groups in two plants.

LAYOFF RATES

	MISSISSIPPI PRODUCTS		PATHFINDER	
EDUCATION GROUPS	White Males	Colored Males	White Males	Colored Males
Under 10 years	.8	1.2	3.2	..
10 years and over	1.4	1.1	2.3	..
Under 6 years	..	1.7	..	2.0
6 years and over	..	1.3	..	4.7

At Mississippi Products, Inc., white males with more education had a higher layoff rate than did those with less education; the opposite was true for colored males. At the Pathfinder Coach Division, on the other hand, white males with more education had a lower layoff rate than did those with less education; here again the experience of colored males was the reverse of that of white males.

5. RURAL-URBAN BACKGROUND

Perhaps the most important comparison for a study in this area is the relative adaptability to an industrial environment of those with rural backgrounds and those with urban backgrounds. For this reason, several approaches to this particular problem were used. In the first case, a comparison was made of the absence rates of those born in rural areas and those born in urban areas. At first glance, this may seem to be a rather unimportant comparison, but if account be taken of the fact that the early years of most of the workers, so important in the formation of habits for later life, were spent in the environment in which they were born, these figures may have some importance. These rates were as follows: except in the case of colored males at the Pathfinder Coach Division and white males at Day-Brite Lighting, Inc., those with rural birth were absent considerably less than those born in urban areas.

ABSENCE RATES

	Mississippi Products		Day-Brite	Pathfinder	
Place of Birth	White Males	Colored Males	White Males	White Males	Colored Males
Rural	3.5	3.0	2.6	1.1	.6
Urban	5.0	4.0	2.0	1.4	.2

A second measure used to ascertain the background of the workers was their residence at the time they applied for jobs in these plants. The following table shows the connection between absenteeism and the rural or urban nature of this place of residence. In the case of both race groups at Mississippi Products, those whose previous residence was rural were absent more than those whose previous residence was urban. This is the reverse of what was found in the case of place of birth and seems to indicate that those who were born in the country and moved to town sometime prior to applying for this job had developed attendance habits which resulted in lower absence rates than those who had not moved to town prior to this application. In the case of Pathfinder Coach Division, the white males whose immediately previous residence was rural and the colored males whose immediately previous residence was urban had lower absence rates than their opposites. This conforms to the data in connection with place of birth for this plant. The experience with white males in the Day-Brite plant was similar to that with white males in the Pathfinder plant.

ABSENCE RATES

PREVIOUS RESIDENCE	MISSISSIPPI PRODUCTS		DAY-BRITE	PATHFINDER	
	White Males	Colored Males	White Males	White Males	Colored Males
Rural	4.5	4.0	2.3	1.0	.5
Urban	3.0	2.0	2.5	1.6	.4

In two plants, the separation rates were computed for people of rural and urban backgrounds. Those born in rural environments had a materially lower separation rate than those born in urban environments.

SEPARATION RATES

PLACE OF BIRTH	MISSISSIPPI PRODUCTS		DAY-BRITE
	White Males	Colored Males	White Males
Rural	10.7	7.0	.8
Urban	13.4	8.4	1.1

When the separation rates for those who lived in rural areas at the time of their application for this job were computed the results were as follows:

SEPARATION RATES

PREVIOUS RESIDENCE	MISSISSIPPI PRODUCTS		DAY-BRITE
	White Males	Colored Males	White Males
Rural	9.8	7.7	1.0
Urban	13.9	8.7	1.2

Again, those with a rural background had consistently lower separation rates than those with an urban background.

In the case of two plants, the output of persons with rural background was compared with that of persons with urban background. The results are shown in the following table:

OUTPUT

	MISSISSIPPI PRODUCTS		DAY-BRITE
	White Males	Colored Males	White Males
PLACE OF BIRTH			
Rural	94.2	99.6	99.3
Urban	91.2	101.2	99.8*
PREVIOUS RESIDENCE			
Rural	102.1	100.4	94.8
Urban	93.0	100.0	97.4
*Less than 3 cases.			

These figures revealed no consistent differences concerning place of birth or previous residence. The differences were small and erratic in direction.

The rates of promotion for those of rural birth were compared with the rates for those of urban birth in two of the plants for the helper-to-operator, trainee-to-operator, and semi-skilled-to-skilled operator promotions. In two cases, those of rural birth were promoted much more rapidly than those of urban birth. In the other case the difference, though in the opposite direction, was negligible.

PROMOTION RATES

	DAY-BRITE	PATHFINDER	
	Helper to Operator	Skill Level 3 to 5	Skill Level 5 to 6
PLACE OF BIRTH	WHITE MALES (Months)	WHITE MALES (Days)	WHITE MALES (Days)
Rural	2.6	40.0	126.0
Urban	3.4	39.5	252.0

The time spent in a classification before promotion by those with rural previous residence as compared with those with urban previous residence is shown in the following table:

PROMOTION RATES

	DAY-BRITE	PATHFINDER		
	Helper to Operator	Skill Level 1 to 2	Skill Level 3 to 5	Skill Level 5 to 6
	WHITE MALES	COLORED MALES	WHITE MALES	WHITE MALES
PREVIOUS RESIDENCE	(Days)	(Days)	(Days)	(Days)
Rural	90.0	51.0	40.0	126.0
Urban	58.5	61.0	40.0	245.0

In the case of the Day-Brite plant, those with urban previous residence spent considerably less time as helper before being promoted to operator. In the case of one of the three promotions studied at Pathfinder, there was no difference between the speed of promotional progress from trainee to operator for white males. In the cases of the promotion of colored males from common labor to trainee or low-skilled production operator and the case of the promotion of white males from semi-skilled to skilled operator, those with rural previous residence showed considerably faster rates of promotion.

In the one plant for which layoff rates were computed by place of birth, the results indicate that management saw fit to lay off persons whose characteristics were those commonly associated with rural rather than with urban birth.

LAYOFF RATES

	MISSISSIPPI PRODUCTS	
	White Males	Colored Males
PLACE OF BIRTH		
Rural	1.2	1.5
Urban	.6	1.2

The rates for those whose residence at the time of application for employment was in a rural area are compared with the rate for those of urban previous residence in the following table:

LAYOFF RATES

	MISSISSIPPI PRODUCTS	
	White	*Colored*
PREVIOUS RESIDENCE	*Males*	*Males*
Rural	1.0	2.0
Urban	1.2	1.2

From the two previous tables, some such conclusion as this might be drawn: Management saw fit to lay off white males who were born in the country and had moved to town before applying for this job and colored males who were born in the country and continued to live in the country.

6. WORK EXPERIENCE GROUPS

Mississippi has been and is a predominantly agricultural area. It therefore becomes important to ascertain whether or not those whose work experience is in agriculture can shift successfully to industrial employment. The group studied was, of course, largely the workers with rural background referred to above.

The groupings used in this connection were: (1) those who had had more work experience in farming than in any other occupational line were contrasted with those whose major experience lay in other fields; (2) those whose most recent job was farming were contrasted with those whose most recent job was in another field; (3) those who had had some experience in farming were contrasted with those who had had no experience in farming; and (4) to a limited extent, those whose only occupational experience was in farming were contrasted with those who had had some experience other than farming.

The following table shows the absence rates for those whose major experience and most recent experience was in farming as against those whose major and most recent experience was other than farming. These figures seem to indicate that the absentee records for people with farming either as major or most recent experience are somewhat inferior to those for people with other occupational backgrounds, except in the case of white males at the Pathfinder plant, where the opposite was true to a limited extent.

ABSENCE RATES

| | MISSISSIPPI PRODUCTS | | DAY-BRITE | PATHFINDER | |
	White Males	Colored Males	White Males	White Males	Colored Males
MAJOR EXPERIENCE					
Farming	4.3	3.5	3.0	1.1	0.6
Other	4.0	2.8	2.7	1.3	.5
MOST RECENT EXPERIENCE					
Farming	4.3	3.4	3.5	1.0	0.5
Other	4.0	3.0	2.6	1.3	.35

It is not unreasonable to expect that occupational background would have an influence on separation rates excluding layoffs, inasmuch as the work habits and regularity are greatly influenced thereby. Life on the farm differs materially from that in industrial employment, and the separation rate excluding layoffs might be expected to reflect satisfaction or dissatisfaction on the part of one or the other of the parties to the employer-employee relationship. The following table compares the separation rates in one plant for those whose major experience was in farming with that for those with other major experience; the separation rates in three plants for those with some farm experience against those with no farm experience; and the rates in one plant for those with only farm experience as against those with other than farming experience.

SEPARATION RATES

| | MISSISSIPPI PRODUCTS | | DAY-BRITE | PATHFINDER | |
	White Males	Colored Males	White Males	White Males	Colored Males
Major experience, farming	10.7	5.9	..	..	..
Major experience, other	17.7	10.7	..	..	..
Some farm experience	10.3	6.2	0.2	1.3	1.1
No farm experience	18.2	12.4	0.3	2.9	2.0
Farm experience only	15.9	8.4	..	..	..
Experience other than farm	9.4	6.7	..	..	..

There was a marked tendency for those with either major farm experience or some farm experience to have lower separation rates than those with other occupational backgrounds. This tendency, however, was sharply reversed when those who had had only farm experience were compared with those who had had some experience other than farming. Here is an apparent contradiction which may have a simple explanation. Those who had had both farm and non-farm experience were able to adjust better to the conditions they found on these jobs than those who had only farm experience and who were finding this first attempt at transition difficult.

When the output of those who had had some farm experience was compared with that of those who had no farm experience, the results were as shown in the following table:

OUTPUT

	Mississippi Products	Day-Brite
	White and Colored Males	White Males
Some farm experience	97.0	104.3
No farm experience	100.1	98.7

The lack of consistency in direction, as well as the smallness of the degree of difference, indicates no close relation between farm experience or lack of it and the capacity to produce in an industrial environment.

The rates of promotional progress for those with the various groupings of farm experience are shown in the following table:

PROMOTION RATES

	Mississippi Products		Day-Brite	Pathfinder		
	Skill Level 6 to 5 White Males (Months)	Skill Level 5 to 4 White Males (Months)	Helper to Operator White Males (Months)	Skill Level 1 to 2 Colored Males (Days)	Skill Level 3 to 5 White Males (Days)	Skill Level 5 to 6 White Males (Days)
Major occupation, farming..	3.9	4.0	..	55	38.2	98.0
Major occupation, other	4.0	4.2	..	71	44.4	134.0
Most recent job, farming ...	4.2	4.0	..	..	36.3	108.5
Most recent job, other	3.8	3.8	..	..	44.2	147.0
Some farm experience	..	1.3	..	39.7	133.0
No farm experience	..	3.4	..	45.8	137.5
Farm experience only	..	..	..	37.5	.. *

*Less than 3 cases.

Those with farm experience in a particular grouping showed somewhat more rapid progress in all cases except that of Mississippi Products, Inc., where employees whose most recent job was in farming showed less rapid progress.

Management's evaluation of persons with farm experience as compared with those without farm experience, as shown by the selection of the workers to be laid off when reduction of force was necessary, is given in the following table for the two plants where this measure was meaningful.

SEPARATION RATES

	MISSISSIPPI PRODUCTS		PATHFINDER	
	White Males	*Colored Males*	*White Males*	*Colored Males*
Major experience, farming	0.7	1.3	..	..
Major experience, other	1.6	2.3	..	..
Some farm experience	.6	1.2	2.5	2.8
No farm experience	1.2	2.2	2.8	2.0
Farm experience only	.7	1.0	..	..
Other than farm experience	.7	3.3	..	..

On the whole it would appear that management, by these actions, expressed a preference for those with farm experience as against those without it, the one exception being colored males at the Pathfinder plant.

It would appear likely that previous experience in manufacturing would tend to promote successful adaptation to employment in these three manufacturing plants. There are, however, certain aspects of Mississippi manufacturing employment which would prevent this generalization from applying. To a very large extent, the workers here dealt with who had manufacturing experience were experienced in logging and lumbering (manufacturing classifications in the Standard Industrial Classification), where the general environment was not particularly similar to that in the large plants studied, and, in many respects, more closely resembled that of farming. Also, much of the manufacturing experience, even outside of logging and lumbering, was in small plants, which have been typical in Mississippi, and which furnished employment differing in important respects from that of the large manufacturing plants here studied.

The absence rates of those with manufacturing experience as either their major occupational experience or as their experience immediately prior to their employment by these firms are shown in the following table:

ABSENCE RATES

	MISSISSIPPI PRODUCTS		DAY-BRITE	PATHFINDER	
	White Males	Colored Males	White Males	White Males	Colored Males
Major experience, manufacturing ...	3.8	2.7	2.9	1.4	0.60
Major experience, other	4.3	3.4	2.7	1.1	.55
Most recent job, manufacturing	4.2	3.3	2.9	1.4	.35
Most recent job, other	4.0	3.2	2.7	1.1	.65

From these figures it would appear that there was no consistent pattern in this connection. There seems, however, some indication that white males with manufacturing experience tended to be absent somewhat more than those with no manufacturing experience.

Separation rates excluding layoffs were computed in one plant for those with major experience in manufacturing as contrasted with those with major experience in other industries, and in all three plants for those with some manufacturing experience as against those with no such experience as shown below.

SEPARATION RATES

	MISSISSIPPI PRODUCTS		DAY-BRITE	PATHFINDER	
	White Males	Colored Males	White Males	White Males	Colored Males
Major experience, manufacturing ...	13.0	7.8	..	..	..
Major experience, other	10.3	6.8	..	..	..
Some manufacturing experience	9.0	6.6	0.9	1.5	2.3
No manufacturing experience	12.0	7.3	1.2	2.6	1.8

Where major experience was involved, those with a manufacturing background (in one plant) had a higher separation rate than those whose major experience lay in other fields. The opposite was true, with one exception, when the separation rate of those with some manufacturing experience was contrasted with the rate for those with no manufacturing experience (in three plants).

In two plants it was possible to compare the separation rate of those who had had experience handling the same material as in the job under study with the rate for those for whom these jobs represented the first experience with this material, woodworking in one case and metalworking in the other. The results are shown by the following figures. It would appear that experience in handling a given material

SEPARATION RATES

| | MISSISSIPPI PRODUCTS | | DAY-BRITE |
	White Males	Colored Males	White Males
With experience on same material	6.1	6.3	0.3
Without experience on same material	11.0	6.9	.9

increased the probability that a performance with the same material would be satisfactory to management and that the work environment was likely to be satisfactory to the employee.

In the case of Mississippi Products, Inc., it was possible to compare the separation rate for those who had worked in manufacturing plants of the same kind with that for those whose work experience did not include furniture manufacture. The results are shown by the following figures. Here again, it appeared that similar manufacturing experience promoted satisfactory adjustment.

SEPARATION RATES

| | MISSISSIPPI PRODUCTS | |
	White Males	Colored Males
With furniture experience	5.3	5.0
Without furniture experience	10.8	6.0

The effect of previous manufacturing experience on the output attained by individuals in a subsequent manufacturing job was investigated and yielded the following results.

OUTPUT

| | MISSISSIPPI PRODUCTS | DAY-BRITE |
	White and Colored Males	White Males
With some manufacturing experience	98.0	97.5
With no manufacturing experience	96.3	102.9

There was no indication of a tendency, since the results were inconsistent in the two plants.

The same thing was true when those with experience handling the same material were compared with those without such experience as shown below.

OUTPUT

	MISSISSIPPI PRODUCTS	DAY-BRITE
	White and Colored Males	White Males
With experience on the same material	99.2	97.2
Without experience on the same material	95.2	99.8

Experience in the same kind of manufacturing employment did not result in a higher output per hour in the case of Mississippi Products Inc., the only plant for which such figures were available. Here the results were as follows:

With furniture experience 97.4

Without furniture experience 98.7

The rate of promotional progress of those falling in the various groupings of manufacturing experience are shown in the table on page 87.

At Pathfinder Coach Division promotion at the lowest skill level, from skill level 1 to skill level 2, which involved colored males, showed no difference in the rate of promotion between those with some manufacturing experience and those with no manufacturing experience. At Pathfinder also, manufacturing experience in any of the groups, including experience in working the same material, appeared to have been a marked advantage in promotion of white males. For the semiskilled jobs falling between these two extremes, no consistent pattern was apparent.

The layoff rates for the various groupings of manufacturing experience in two of the plants appear below. In the case of Mississippi Products, Inc., previous manufacturing experience, whether as major experience or as part of the previous occupational experience seemed to have been a disadvantage in the eyes of management when selecting

PROMOTION RATES

	MISSISSIPPI PRODUCTS		DAY-BRITE		PATHFINDER	
	Skill Level 6 to 5 WHITE MALES (Months)	*Skill Level 5 to 4* WHITE MALES (Months)	*Helper to Operator* WHITE MALES (Months)	*Skill Level 1 to 2* COLORED MALES (Days)	*Skill Level 3 to 5* WHITE MALES (Days)	*Skill Level 5 to 6* WHITE MALES (Days)
Major experience, manufacturing	3.0	6.5	..	..	36.0	118.5
Major experience, other	4.1	4.6	..	..	40.0	147.0
Most recent job, manufacturing	3.3	3.0	..	..	42.0	81.5
Most recent job, other	4.0	5.2	..	..	39.0	214.0
Some manufacturing experience	..	..	3.3	60.0	43.9	106.0
No manufacturing experience	..	..	1.8	60.0	39.1	219.0
Experience with same material	..	..	2.7	..	38.2	87.5
No experience with same material	..	..	2.6	..	43.7	162.5

LAYOFF RATES

	MISSISSIPPI PRODUCTS		PATHFINDER	
	White Males	Colored Males	White Males	Colored Males
Major experience, manufacturing	1.8	2.1	..	..
Major experience, other	.9	1.3	..	..
Some manufacturing experience	.9	1.3	2.3	0.5
No manufacturing experience	.8	1.3	3.2	6.5
Experience with same material	.6	1.3	..	..
No experience with same material	.9	.9	..	..
Furniture manufacturing experience	.6	1.7	..	..
No furniture manufacturing experience..	.8	1.3	..	..

those workers to be laid off to make a necessary reduction in work force. However, experience working in the same material or in the same kind of manufacturing operation was advantageous to white males and disadvantageous to colored males. In the case of the Pathfinder Coach Division, those of both races with some manufacturing experience had lower layoff rates than those without such experience.

VII

CONCLUSION

A SUMMARY OF A STUDY such as this requires re-evaluation of the data in terms of its adequacy in attaining the goals which were set. The goals in this study were two in number: first, to examine the availability of labor for these new industrial plants and, second, to examine the adaptability of that labor to industrial employment. The first goal was approached by examining the extent of recruitment efforts and the numbers and nature of the workers who applied for jobs. The second goal was approached in two ways: first, by comparing the adaptability of Mississippi workers to industrial employment with that of workers in more highly industrialized sections of the country and, second, by comparing the degree to which the various characteristic groups proved to be able to adjust themselves to an industrial environment. Particular emphasis was placed on discovering which groups, if any, tended to make unsatisfactory employees to the end that some estimate of the potential labor force in Mississippi might be made.

One of the reasons frequently cited to explain why marked industrialization in Mississippi is unlikely has been the widespread incidence of debilitating diseases. Investigation shows, however, that in the past few years and particularly since the end of World War II there has been a marked decrease in the prevalence of such diseases in Mississippi. It would appear that the ill health or lack of initiative, the undependability and the lack of ambition, which sometimes accompanied these disabilities and which would in fact make the acceptance of industrial discipline difficult, has come to play a minor role inasmuch as the number of people affected has been reduced remarkably.

Only a limited number of the products of a plant could be used to compare the output of Mississippi plants with that of plants located in other areas, since comparison was possible only where the units produced were or could be made identical and were produced by identical methods. For a discussion of the limitations of the data used in comparing different characteristic groups, see Chapter VI.

1. AVAILABILITY OF LABOR

In all three plants management was able to obtain the necessary labor force with only limited investment of effort and expense in the recruiting program. This limited program was sufficient to attract not only unskilled labor but also semi-skilled and skilled machine operators and skilled maintenance men and craftsmen (including tool and die makers), all being found available in the local labor market.

2. COMPARISON OF MISSISSIPPI AND NON-MISSISSIPPI WORKERS

The data presented here did not indicate a high absentee rate in the Mississippi plants, though only limited comparative information in non-Mississippi plants were available for the period covered.

After the breaking-in period, the turnover rate in these plants was somewhat below the average for the nation in plants in similar industries as reported by the Bureau of Labor Statistics. In one plant it was lower from the very beginning.

Accident frequency and severity rates were obtained in two of the three plants. In one case, they ran below the average rate for the industry, except for the initial breaking-in period, indicating that the workers responded well to safety training and were not particularly accident-prone. In the other case, the frequency rate was above the national average, though the severity rate compared favorably with the national average.

No material difference appeared to exist between the output per man-hour in the Mississippi industrial plants and those in other areas. In one of the cases studied, the Mississippi plant had a slightly higher productivity than did the non-Mississippi plant; in another case the advantage in productivity of the Mississippi plant was so small as to be negligible, while in the third case a substantial advantage in productivity lay with the non-Mississippi plant. On the basis of these conflicting data, no generalization as to regional advantage in productivity seemed justified.

3. COMPARISONS AMONG MISSISSIPPI WORKERS

This matter has been treated in detail in Chapter VI and at this point requires only a broad summarization.

The data indicate that Mississippi white males, to the extent that they are here represented, make satisfactory industrial employees. This seems to be true regardless of age or education or any of the other characteristics discussed in Chapter VI. This means that a substantial segment of the white males in Mississippi could be used successfully to man a very material expansion in Mississippi industrialization.

The data also indicate that Mississippi colored males make excellent industrial employees. This is particularly true in connection with the measures of dependability and steadiness, where doubt concerning the ability of colored males to accept the discipline of industrial employment has often been expressed. Here again the conclusion applies to all the characteristic groups of colored males represented in the data. This seems to assure that this considerable segment of the Missisippi population can be considered a part of the potential industrial labor force. The above is true with regard to colored males holding unskilled and semi-skilled jobs. The data on colored males in skilled jobs were too limited to support any generalization.

The limited data on white females as production workers indicate that this group, making up a considerable segment of the Mississippi population, adjusts well to industrial employment and produces a record of successful performance. Since the data in this connection were so limited, a breakdown of this group of workers comparable to that for the two previous groups was impossible, and no information was available on the various segments of the sex-race group.

On the whole, the evidence seems to support a rather optimistic forecast of Mississippi's ability to man the industrial plants which would be present in a highly-industrialized state. In no case, where a plant started hiring members of the three sex-race groups, did experience cause them to change their minds and to employ materially more or less, fractionally, of the workers falling in each of the sex-race groups. In addition, all important parts of any of these sex-race groups who were ever hired by these plants were still represented at the time of the study. Though the various groups seemed to excel in certain aspects of performance, no consistency appeared which would indicate a material superiority or inferiority of any segment of the population insofar as this study has been able to deal with these various segments. That is to say that, apparently, a rather large fraction of the population of Mississippi is capable of adapting itself to an industrial environment.

APPENDICES

APPENDIX A

WORK FORCE AT MISSISSIPPI PRODUCTS, INC., ACCORDING TO SKILL LEVEL OF EMPLOYMENT AS OF AUGUST, 1951

At the time this study was made Mississippi Products, Inc., had only 586 production workers. This was a low point in employment, due to a slackness in the market for the finished product. These 586 workers fell in job classifications which the job evaluation plan at Mississippi Products, Inc., arranged in seven different skill levels according to the amount of skill required to perform the various jobs. Skill level 7 was composed of common labor classifications and covered 147 colored males. Skill level 6 was composed of classifications which might be called the higher unskilled jobs, and was also used as the hiring-in level for machine operator, assembly, and finishing trainees. It was made up of three sex-race groups. There were 42 white males, thirteen white females, and 87 colored males in these classifications. Skill level 5 included trained mill machine operators who could not do even simple set-ups on the machines they operated. It also included minor assembly and minor finishing classifications. It was composed of 39 white males, nine white females, and thirty colored males, for a total of 78 persons. Skill level 4 was composed of mill machine operators capable of doing simple set-ups, advanced assemblers, advanced finishers, craftsmen's helpers, and a more skilled type of salvagers of damaged end products. It was composed of 92 white males, four white females, and eight colored males. Skill level 3 was composed of mill machine operators capable of performing complicated set-ups and skilled finish and cabinet repairers. It included 71 white males, four white females, and no colored males. Skill level 2 was composed of second-class maintenance men and craftsmen and finish patchers of advanced skill. It included fourteen white males and one white female.

Skill level 1 was composed of first-class maintenance men and crafts-men. It included 25 white males.

A summarization of the information concerning the workers in these seven skill levels can be best presented in graphic form. The charts which follow, it will be noted, are proportional bar graphs which show the percentage of all employed in each skill level who had the indicated characteristic.

Chart 12 reveals the race-sex compositions of the various skill levels. It will be noted that the lowest job classification is occupied entirely by colored males and that colored men make up a rapidly decreasing proportion of the next three skill levels. No colored males fall in any of the three highest skill levels. White females fall in skill levels 6 through 2, making up a larger per cent of the total employment in skill level 3 than in any other level. White males make up a relatively small proportion of skill level 6 and an increasing proportion of the higher levels up to 100 per cent in skill level 1.

Because of the non-competing character of the sex-race groups at Mississippi Products, Inc., each group will be described separately.

Chart 13 shows the median age and the range of ages for each sex-race group. There is no apparent connection between age and skill level for white females, colored males, and white males below skill level 3. For white males above skill level 3, there is an upward trend in median age and in minimum age as we move toward the higher skill levels.

Chart 14 indicates that there was little connection between the amount of formal education and the skill levels at which production workers were employed at Mississippi Products, Inc.

Chart 15 indicates the proportion of single, married, divorced, widowed or separated in each sex-race group in each skill level. There appears to be a tendency for divorced, widowed or separated persons to make up a somewhat larger proportion of the lower skill levels, and the same is true to a limited extent, of single persons.

Chart 16 indicates the place of birth of the production employees. It is notable that few of the white men were born in Jackson or Hinds County, the majority being born in Mississippi counties outside of those contiguous to Hinds. A small number were born in the South outside Mississippi and a very small number outside the South. Native Mississippians made up 75 per cent of the workers in skill level 1. A somewhat larger proportion of the white females and colored males were born within the Jackson area than was the case for white males. A majority were born in Hinds County and contiguous counties.

As indicated in Chart 17, by the time they applied for employment at Mississippi Products, Inc., a considerable migration of these workers had occurred toward Jackson, presumably for the purpose of obtaining jobs with prior employers in the Jackson area. It will be noted that the concentration in Hinds and surrounding counties was lowest for white males and highest for colored males, indicating perhaps a somewhat lower degree of mobility of colored workers prior to taking these positions at Mississippi Products, Inc.

Chart 18 indicates the location of the residence of the labor force at the time this study was made. A considerable majority lived in Jackson or Hinds County, with a sizeable minority in contiguous counties. Only a small minority lived farther away.

Chart 19 shows the major experience of the persons comprising this labor force. Note that for all skill levels up to and including skill level 2, for white males, farming experience was well represented, followed by manufacturing experience, but there is no apparent relation between experience in these two categories and the skill level occupied. In skill level 1, however, persons with farming experience were relatively unimportant, while those with manufacturing experience made up a majority, followed in importance by construction and service experience. For the white females, farming experience was fairly rare, most experience being in manufacturing trade or service industries. For the colored males, farming experience was more common than for either of the other two groups, and the proportion of those with farming as major experience was higher in skill level 4 than in any of the lower skill levels. Next to farming, experience in manufacturing was the most common type of occupational background for the colored males.

Chart 20 shows the skill classification occupied by these persons during their major occupational experience. For the white males, there was roughly a decline in the proportion having unskilled experience as we move from lower to higher skill levels in present employment. The proportion of semi-skilled in skill levels 6 through 3 showed no discernible trend. In skill level 2, however, the previously semi-skilled workers were a majority of all cases. In skill level 1, few persons of unskilled major experience were present. A somewhat larger, but still small, group were those whose experience was semi-skilled. A majority of those in skill level 1 was made up of persons who occupied skilled positions or supervisory positions in the industry of their major experience. For white females, clerical and sales experience was more important than for the other sex-race groups; but those with experience in semi-skilled occupations represented a majority in three of the four skill levels occupied by women. For colored males, the proportion with unskilled experience diminished and the proportion with semi-skilled experience tended to increase from skill level 7 to skill level 4.

Chart 21 concerns the veteran status of these employees. For white males, with the exception of classification 2, there was a slight tendency for the proportion of veterans to decline in the higher skill levels. This tendency was more marked in skill levels 3 and 1 where it may have reflected the ages of the workers rather than the connection between lack of skill and military experience. Skill level 2, containing only a few persons, represented to some extent a training classification for skilled workers. There seemed to be little connection between veteran status and the skill levels occupied by colored males.

Chart 22 indicates the industry in which these people worked immediately prior to employment at Mississippi Products, Inc. For white males, farming was represented somewhat lightly even in skill levels 3 and below, very lightly in skill level 2, and not at all in skill level 1. A comparison with Chart 19 would indicate that considerable industry-ward movement had taken place by the time of employment at Mississippi Products, Inc. Manufacturing experience was well represented here, especially in skill levels 2 and 1, while a considerable number of white males in all skill levels, and especially in the two highest, transferred to Mississippi Products, Inc., from the construction industry. The immediately prior job, as well as major experience, for white females was, in a vast majority of cases, in manufacturing, trade, or service. For colored males, experience in manufacturing was common, but it is interesting to note an upward tendency in those with experience in service industries as we move from lower to higher skill levels, and to note that in skill level 4, the highest level occupied by colored males, manufacturing experience played a relatively small part while farming experience was relatively more important. More

than one-third of the colored males in skill level 4 transferred directly
from the farm to this job.

Chart 23 indicates the skill level at which these workers were employed immediately prior to their transfer to Mississippi Products,
Inc. A considerable number of the white males in skill levels 6 through
2 came directly from unskilled jobs, and there appeared to be no discernible connection between the level of skill at which they were employed in previous jobs and the skill level attained at Mississippi
Products, Inc. The same could be said of persons with semi-skilled
experience in these five skill levels, but is not true of those in skill
level 1, over 75 per cent of whom held skilled jobs prior to being hired
by Mississippi Products, Inc. Few white females came to these jobs
from unskilled positions, most having been in semi-skilled jobs, with
a sizeable minority having been clerks or salespeople. Most of the
colored males transferred to this company from unskilled jobs, with a
sizeable minority having held semi-skilled work.

This then is a description of the labor force that Mississippi Products, Inc., built up in the first five years of operation. It is not a
description of the maximum force which had been employed, but
rather of the residue following a considerable layoff; in other words,
this is a description of that portion of the maximum force which the
company preferred to keep on its payroll and which it had succeeded
in keeping on its payroll.

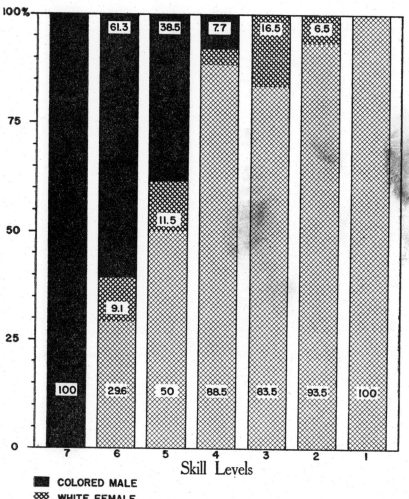

CHART 12. Sex and Race Groups as Per Cent of Total Employed in Each Skill Group

Skill Levels

■ COLORED MALE
▨ WHITE FEMALE
▨ WHITE MALE

CHART 13. Median Age and Age Range in Each Skill Level for Three Sex-race Groups

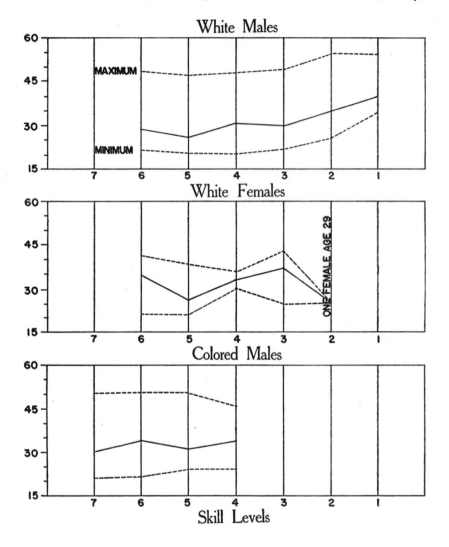

CHART 14. Median Education and Education Range in Each Skill Level for Three Sex-race Groups

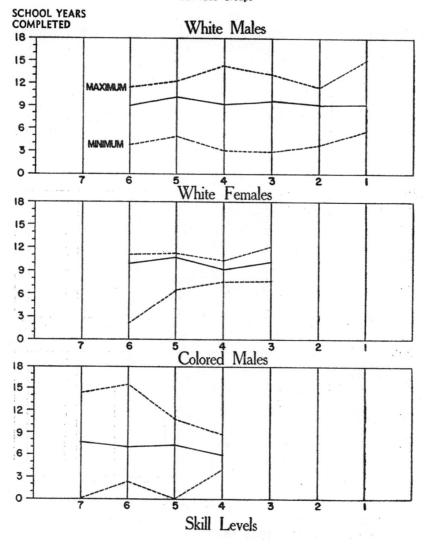

SCHOOL YEARS COMPLETED

Skill Levels

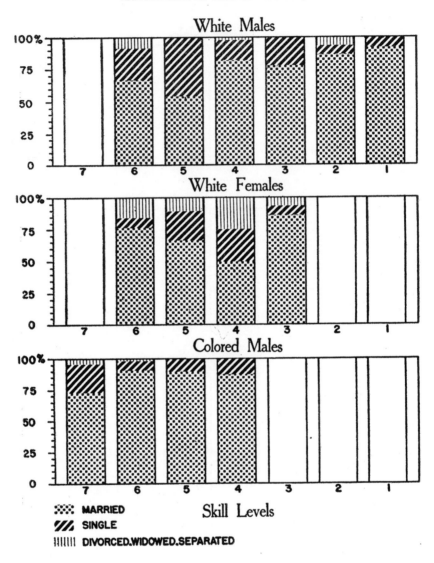

CHART 15. Number in Each Marital Status Group as a Per Cent of Total Employment in Each Skill Level for Three Sex-race Groups

CHART 16. Number in Each Place-of-birth Group as a Per Cent of Total Employment in Each Skill Level for Three Sex-race Groups

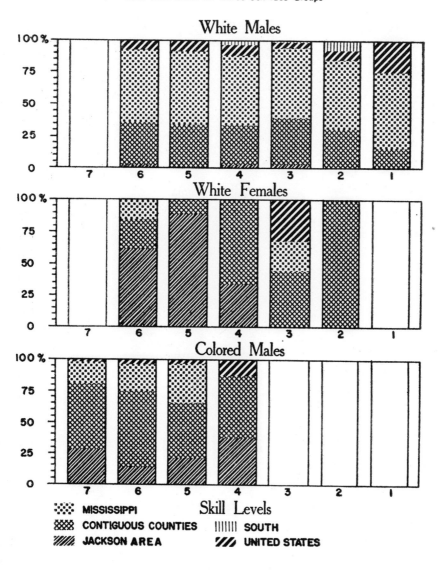

CHART 17. Number in Each Residence-when-employed Group as a Per Cent of Total
Employment in Each Skill Level for Three Sex-race Groups

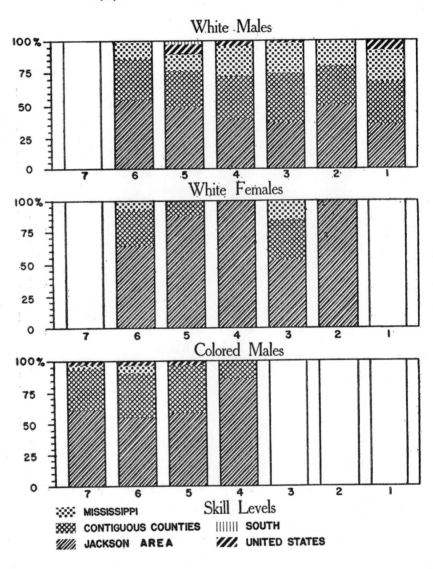

CHART 18. Number in Each Present-residence Group as a Per Cent of Total Employment in Each Skill Level for Three Sex-race Groups

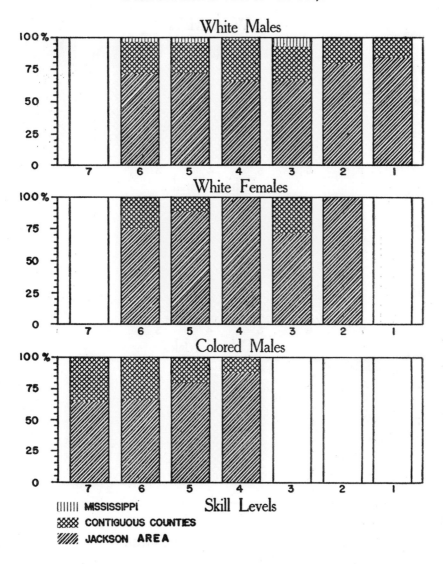

CHART 19. Number in Each Major-experience Group as a Per Cent of Total Employment in Each Skill Level for Three Sex-race Groups

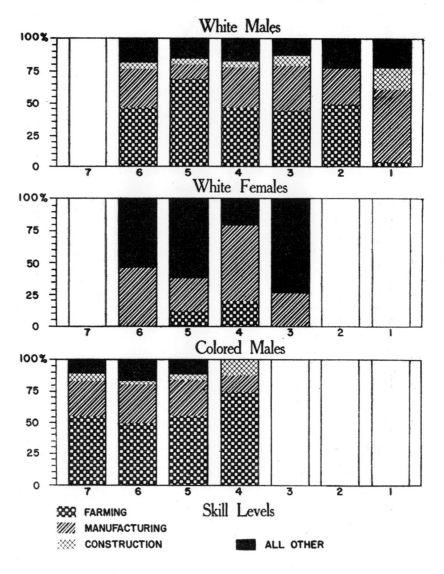

CHART 20. Number in Each Major-skill-level Group as a Per Cent of Total Employment in Each Skill Level for Three Sex-race Groups

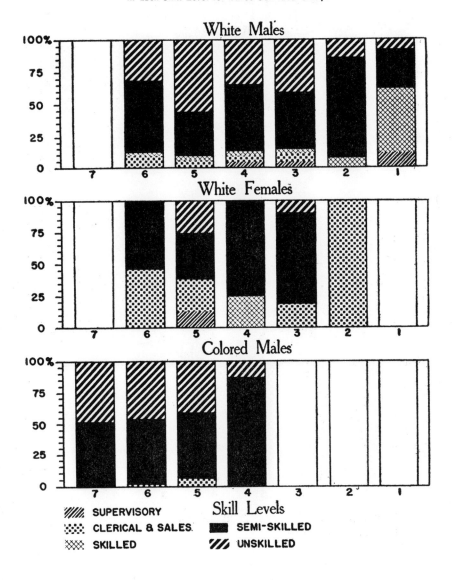

White Males

White Females

Colored Males

Skill Levels

▨ SUPERVISORY
⠿ CLERICAL & SALES   ■ SEMI-SKILLED
▨ SKILLED   ▨ UNSKILLED

CHART 21. Number in Each Veteran-status Group as a Per Cent of Total Employment in
Each Skill Level for Three Sex-race Groups

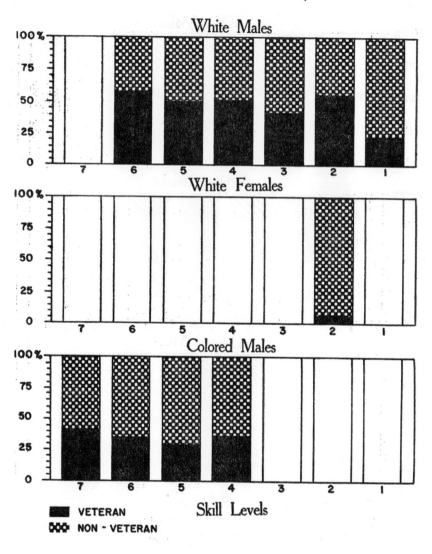

Skill Levels

CHART 22. Number in Each Most-recent-job Group as a Per Cent of Total Employment in Each Skill Level for Three Sex-race Groups

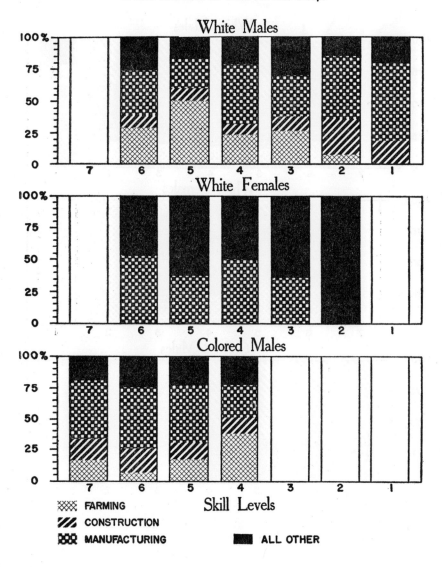

FARMING

CONSTRUCTION

MANUFACTURING

ALL OTHER

CHART 23. Number in Each Most-recent-skill Group as a Per Cent of Total Employment in Each Skill Level for Three Sex-race Groups

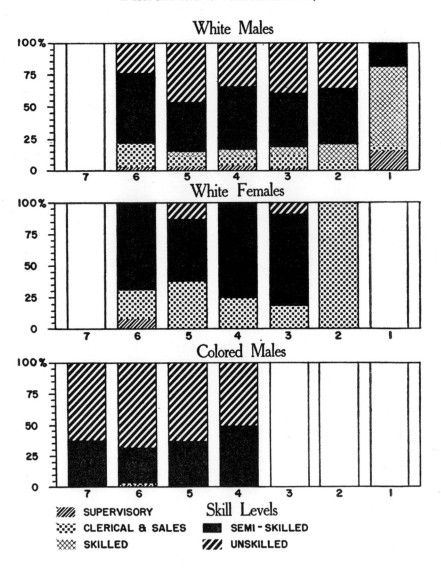

APPENDIX B

WORK FORCE AT DAY-BRITE LIGHTING, INC., ACCORDING TO SKILL LEVEL OF EMPLOYMENT AS OF MARCH, 1952

The 104 workers at Day-Brite Lighting, Inc., were divided into 28 classifications, which were, in turn, divided roughly into five skill levels by the job evaluation plan made at the time the Tupelo plant began operations. Later the plan was changed somewhat by the management in view of its experience in production. The following is a list of the job classifications showing their division into skill levels 1 through 5.

SKILL LEVEL	JOB TITLES
No. 1	Laborer
	Laborer, paint
	Utility stock handler
	Scrap baler and collector
	Ship laborer
	Stock handler
	Box maker
	Utility driver
No. 2	Press helper
	Shear helper
	Assembler
	Wireman
	Packer
	Lift truck operator
No. 3	Maintenance helper
	Press operator
	Shear operator
	Spray painter, 2nd class
	Painter, 2nd class
No. 4	Maintenance
	Spray painter, 1st class
	Painter, 1st class
	Finish painter
	Leadman
	Tool room specialist
	Die setter
No. 5	Maintenance leadman
	Tool and die maker

The following charts show the characteristics of the workers in the job classifications within each of the skill levels:

Chart 24 shows the median age and age range for the workers falling in each skill level. It indicates little variation in the class of job held by the various age groups.

Chart 25 indicates the median educational level of the workers in each skill level. Little difference in educational requirements of jobs at different skill levels is indicated except in the case of skill level 5 where the median education was somewhat higher. Of interest is the minimum educational qualifications of the different groups. The minimum education increased as the skill of the job increased.

Chart 26 shows the marital status of the workers in each skill level. None of these workers was divorced, separated, or widowed. There seems to be a tendency for single workers to fall more in the highest skill level and in the lowest skill level than in those requiring moderate skill. Those in skill level 1 include many workers whose youth explains why they are neither skilled nor married.

Chart 27 shows the proportion of the workers in each skill level born in different geographical locations with relation to Tupelo. In general, with the exception of skill level 4, the higher the skill level the larger the proportion of workers born outside Mississippi. The proportion of those born in Lee County was greater in the higher skill levels, while the proportion of those born in contiguous counties was greater in the lower skill levels.

Chart 28 indicates the place of residence of the workers in the different skill levels just prior to accepting this job. With one exception, the proportion of workers whose previous residence was in Tupelo was decreased as the level of skill increased, while the proportion of those who resided in Lee County was higher for the higher skill levels. Those who previously lived in contiguous counties occupy only the three lower skill levels.

Chart 29 shows the current residence of the workers in the various skill levels. In the main, the higher the skill level the greater the proportion of the workers living in Tupelo. Perhaps the higher earnings of these workers permit residence in the city. Those who lived in contiguous counties at the time of the study appear in only the three lowest skill levels and even there the proportion represented decreases as the skill level increases.

Chart 30 shows the proportion of the workers in each skill level who have had their major occupational experience in each of the various industries. Those with farming as major experience compose about the same proportion of the workers in each skill level and the same is true of those with manufacturing experience except in skill level 5 where the proportion with manufacturing as major experience is materially larger. Except in the case of skill level 1, those with experience outside farming, construction, and manufacturing became a smaller proportion of all the workers in each succeedingly higher skill level.

Chart 31 indicates the skill classification of the job held during major experience, expressed as a fraction of all workers in each present skill level. For the lowest three skill levels, the proportion who held unskilled jobs during their major experience increases as the skill level of the present job increases. In the first four skill levels, former experience on skilled jobs appears to have less influence on the present skill level than would be expected, but only those whose major experience was skilled held jobs in the highest skill level.

Chart 32 shows the proportion of the workers in each skill level whose last previous job was in each of the various industries. With the exception of skill level 4, the proportion having had manufacturing experience is higher for the higher skill levels. Except for skill level 1, the proportion with experience in farming, construction, and manufacturing increased as the skill level increased. None of the workers had transferred directly from farming to a job in skill level 5.

Chart 33 shows the skill category of the most recently held job for the various proportions of the workers making up the various present skill levels. It is notable that there is little consistency between the skill level of the most recent job and the skill level of the present job. Previously unskilled workers are found in all present skill levels and, with the exception of skill level five, workers who held skilled jobs are about as important a fraction of the workers in the low skill levels as in the high.

Chart 34 shows the veteran status of the workers in each skill level. There is a slightly larger proportion with military service in the higher skill levels than in the lower.

Chart 35 indicates the proportion in each skill level who had occupational training of some kind outside the public schools and the proportion who had not. Except in the case of skill level 1, the proportion with occupational training increases as the skill level increases.

CHART 24. Median Age and Age-range in Each Skill Level

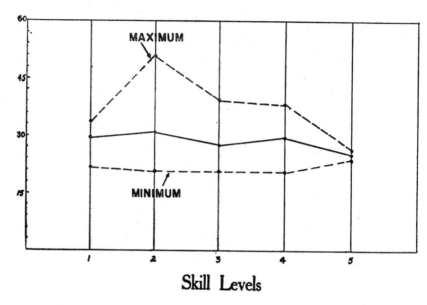

Skill Levels

CHART 25. Median Education and Education-range in Each Skill Level

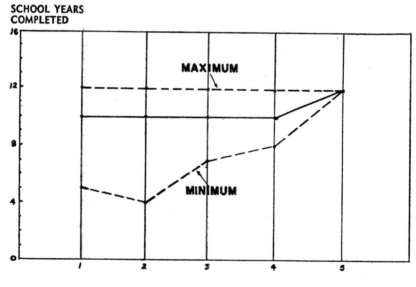

Skill Levels

CHART 26. Number in Each Marital Status Group as a Per Cent of Total Employment in Each Skill Level

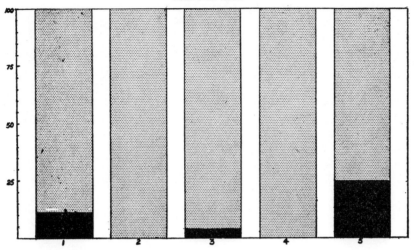

Skill Levels

MARRIED
SINGLE

CHART 27. Number in Each Place-of-birth Group as a Per Cent of Total Employment in Each Skill Level

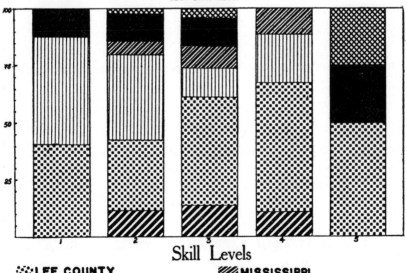

Skill Levels

LEE COUNTY   MISSISSIPPI
CONTIGUOUS AREA   UNITED STATES
SOUTH   TUPELO

CHART 28. Number in Each Residence-when-employed Group as a Per Cent of Total Employment in Each Skill Level

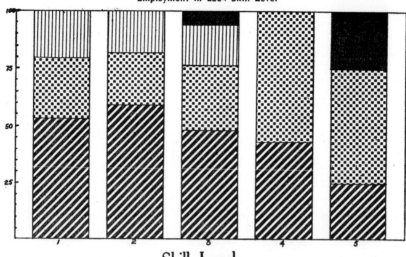

Skill Levels

▧ TUPELO ||||| CONTIGUOUS AREA
⋮⋮⋮ LEE COUNTY   ▨ SOUTH

CHART 29. Number in Each Present-residence Group as a Per Cent of Total Employment in Each Skill Level

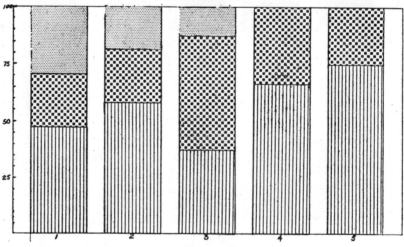

||||| TUPELO   Skill Levels
⋮⋮⋮ LEE COUNTY
▨ CONTIGUOUS AREA

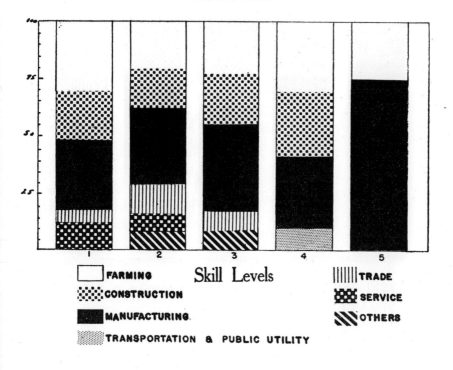

CHART 30. Number in Each Major-experience Group as a Per Cent of Total Employment in Each Skill Level

CHART 31. Number in Each Major-skill-level Group as a Per Cent of Total Employment
in Each Skill Level

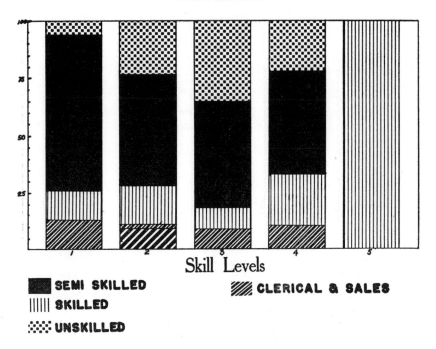

Skill Levels

■ SEMI SKILLED   ▨ CLERICAL & SALES
‖‖‖‖ SKILLED
∷∷ UNSKILLED

CHART 32. Number in Each Most-recent-job Group as a Per Cent of Total Employment
in Each Skill Level

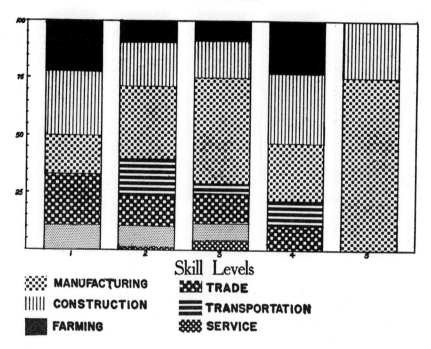

CHART 33. Number in Each Most-recent-skill group as a Per Cent of Total Employment in Each Skill Level

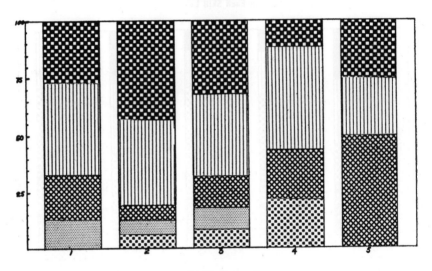

Skill Levels

▨ SKILLED   ▨ CLERICAL & SALES
▨ SEMI SKILLED   ▨ SUPERVISORY
▨ UNSKILLED

CHART 34. Number in Each Veteran-status Group as a Per Cent of Total Employment in
Each Skill Level

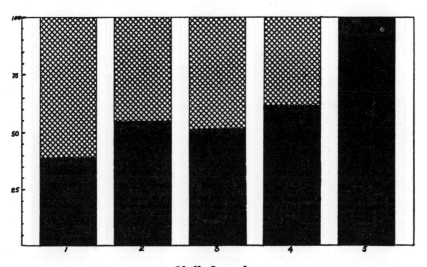

Skill Levels

VETERANS

NON VETERANS

CHART 35. Number in Each Technical-training Group as a Per Cent of Total Employment in Each Skill Level

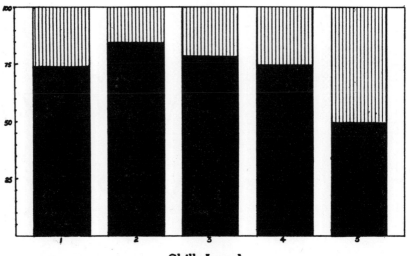

Skill Levels

||||||| WITHOUT TECHNICAL TRAINING

███ WITH TECHNICAL TRAINING

APPENDIX C

WORK FORCE AT PATHFINDER COACH DIVISION, ACCORDING TO SKILL LEVEL OF EMPLOYMENT AS OF NOVEMBER, 1952

There were 309 workers in the Pathfinder plant at the time of this study. A firm of industrial engineers had designed the job evaluation plan, which classified occupations in this plant into seven groups according to skill requirements. Groups 1 and 2 were composed of common laborers and trainees for the less skilled production operations. Skill level 1 had four white males and thirteen colored males; and skill level 2 had seven white males, seven white females, and eight colored males. Groups 3, 4, and 5 included the semi-skilled operators, trainees for the more skilled jobs, and some inspectors and pool leaders in less skilled operations. These were comprised as follows: skill level 3 had 31 white males, one white female and ten colored males; skill level 4 had 27 white males and four colored males; skill level 5 had 109 white males and eight colored males.

Groups 6 and 7 included skilled workers and the pool leaders in the higher skilled operations. There were 67 white males and one colored male in skill level 6, and twelve white males in skill level 7.

Chart 36 shows the percentage distribution of the sex-race groups in the seven skill levels. It will be noted that white males were represented in all skill levels and made up an increasingly larger proportion of total employment as the degree of skill increased until finally, at the highest skill level, only white males are found. Colored males were found in all save the highest skill level and represented a decreasing proportion of total employment as the degree of skill increased. White females were employed only in skill levels 2 and 3, with only one woman in the latter group. There were no colored female production workers.

Chart 37 shows the age distribution for white males and colored males in the various skill levels. Because of the small number of white female production workers no attempt was made to analyze further the relation of their personal characteristics to the skill levels they occupied. In the case of white men, the most notable features were the small range of ages in the lowest skill level and the relatively high median age in that skill level. This was in contrast to the wide range of ages and low median age in skill level 2. Skill level 1 jobs tended to be dead-end unskilled labor jobs while those in skill level 2 were more likely to be stepping stones to higher paid work. For the semi-skilled and skilled white jobs, age seemed to play no important part inasmuch as there was little variation in the median age and a relatively slight narrowing of the age range as the degree of skill increased. For colored males variations in the median ages in the different skill levels were small. Perhaps the most notable feature of this chart is the consistently narrowing range of ages as skill requirements increase.

The range of education and median education of employees at various skill levels is shown in Chart 38. For white males median education was in an upward trend to skill level 4 and on a plateau beyond skill level 4. Also the range was smaller for unskilled and skilled classifications than for the semi-skilled. For colored males there seemed to be no consistent relation between median education and skill level.

Chart 39 shows the marital status of the workers at various skill levels and indicates no particular relation between the two for white males. Single colored men were to be found in only the three lowest skill levels.

Chart 40 indicates the division between rural (towns under 2500 population) and urban places of birth of workers in different skill levels. For white males there seemed to be a tendency for the urban-born to constitute a larger proportion of the total in the unskilled and skilled classifications and smaller proportion in the semi-skilled jobs.

Chart 41 shows the distribution of workers according to their residence, rural or urban, at the time they applied for a job in the Pathfinder plant. With the exception of skill level 2, the pattern for white males was quite similar to that established in Chart 40. For colored males the pattern changed considerably from that established in considering the place of birth of the workers. Here urban residents occupied a much more important proportion of the semi-skilled jobs than was the case with regard to place of birth, and with the exception of skill level 1 the proportion of urban workers increased as the skill requirements increased.

Chart 42 shows the present residence of workers in the various skill levels. All white males and colored males in skill levels 1 and 2, the unskilled jobs, resided in Kosciusko or Attala County. In skill level 7, where there were no Negroes, all workers also resided in Kosciusko or Attala County. It was in the semi-skilled classifications and in skill level 6 that workers were found with residences in more distant location, i.e., contiguous counties and elsewhere in Mississippi. These data concerning colored males were somewhat distorted by the fact that certain colored workers who listed their residence as Greenwood, Mississippi, some 75 miles from Kosciusko, did not drive from their residences to the plant daily but usually spent the work-week nights in Kosciusko and might be considered residents.

Chart 43 shows the major experience of persons in the various skill levels. For white males it is notable that from skill level 1 to skill level 7 the proportion of persons with major experience in farming decreased as skill level increased, and that the proportion with manufacturing experience increased over the whole range of skill levels. For colored males, no consistent pattern with regard to major experience was apparent.

The relation between the skill level at which the workers functioned in the industry of their major experience and their present skill level is shown in Chart 44. For white males the proportion of workers with major experience in skilled jobs increased markedly for job classifications requiring a higher degree of skill. No workers with unskilled major experience were to be found in the unskilled jobs or in skill level 7. The semi-skilled experience of the workers in skill levels 1 and 2 consisted largely of experience as tenant farmers, while semi-skilled experience represented in skill level 7 was mainly non-farming experience. For purposes of this study farm laborers were considered as unskilled, tenant farmers as semi-skilled, and farm owner-operators as skilled workers. No pattern of relationship emerged concerning the skill level during major experience and the present skill level of colored males, indicating that the economy had not tested the skill potentialities of these workers.

Chart 45 indicates the industry in which these workers held jobs immediately prior to the acceptance of employment in the Pathfinder plant. For white males, those who came directly from farming operations constituted a majority of the unskilled workers (skill levels 1 and 2). For the skill levels above these, farmers represented a much smaller fraction of the total. Workers with experience in manufacturing as their more recent job constituted a very small per cent of the unskilled workers but a larger percentage of the semi-skilled and skilled workers. In neither of these cases, however, was there any consistent variation among those with farming or manufacturing experience in the skill levels above 3, except that in skill level 7 the percentage of those with recent farm experience was very small. Manufacturing experience was relatively rare among colored males holding the unskilled jobs and more frequent among those holding semi-skilled jobs. Workers transferring from the construction industry held jobs among the first three skill levels only. No apparent relation between recent farming and skill level was indicated by these data.

Chart 46 shows the relation between the skill level of the most recently held job and the skill level in this plant. As was the case with the skill level in major experience, the white male workers in skill levels 1 and 2 came predominantly from semi-skilled jobs. (See explanation above.) For skill levels 3 to 7 the proportion represented by workers who most recently held unskilled jobs declined as the skill involved in the present job increased. With the exception of skill level 3, the proportion of those coming from skilled jobs increased as the skill of the present job increased. Here again, as in the previous case, the data on colored males revealed no particular pattern.

Chart 47 reveals the extent to which the workers in each skill level had had technical training outside of public school and on-the-job training. For both white and colored males, there was an upward trend in the proportion having such training from skill level 1 to the highest skill level occupied. Part of the explanation for the relatively high proportion of Negroes with technical training lies in the satisfactory cooperation which the management of the plant was able to establish with a veterans training school in Greenwood, Mississippi, the graduates of which the management of the plant considered excellent employees.

CHART 36. Sex and Race Groups as Per Cent of Total Employment in Each Skill Group

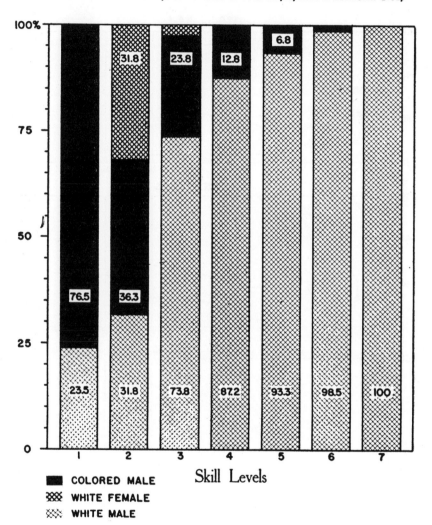

CHART 37. Median Age and Age Range in Each Skill Level for Sex-race Groups

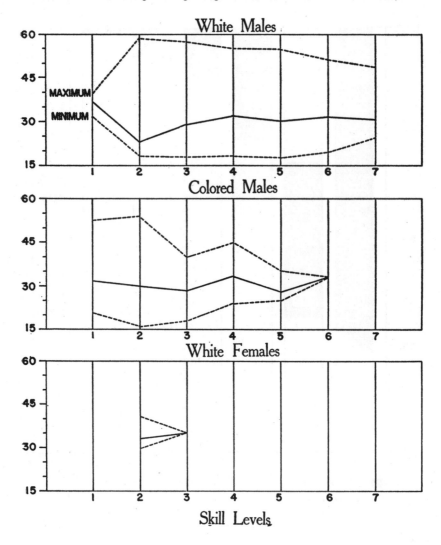

CHART 38. Median Education and Education Range in Each Skill Level for Three Sex-race Groups

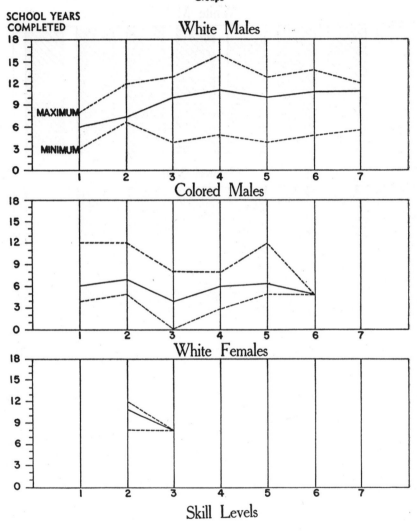

SCHOOL YEARS
COMPLETED

Skill Levels

CHART 39. Number in Each Marital Status Group as a Per Cent of Total Employment in Each Skill Level for Three Sex-race Groups

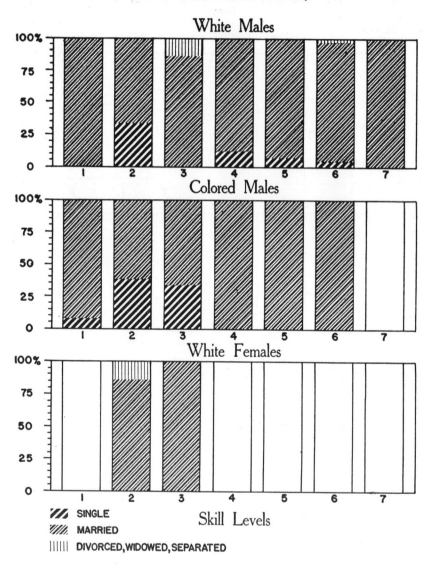

CHART 40. Number in Each Place-of-birth Group as a Per Cent of Total Employment in Each Skill Level for Three Sex-race Groups

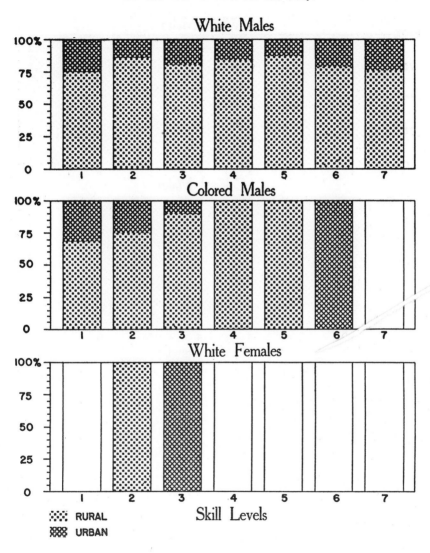

White Males

Colored Males

White Females

Skill Levels

RURAL
URBAN

CHART 41. Number in Each Residence-when-employed Group as a Per Cent of Total Employment in Each Skill Level for Three Sex-race Groups

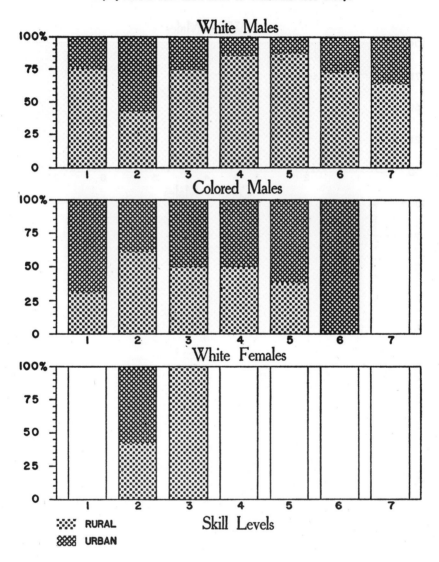

CHART 42. Number in Each Present Residence Group as a Per Cent of Total Employment in Each Skill Level for Three Sex-race Groups

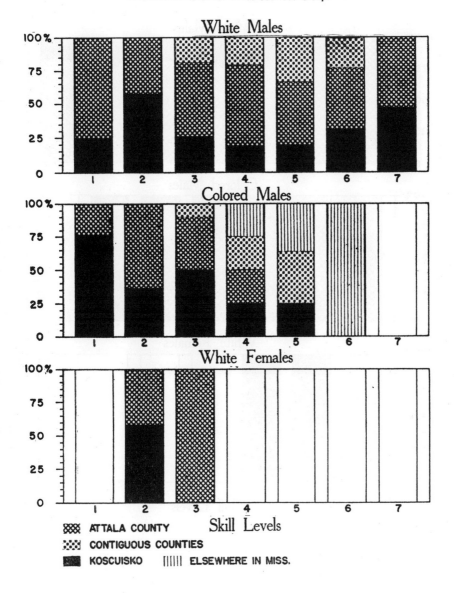

CHART 43. Number in Each Major Experience Group as a Per Cent of Total Employment
in Each Skill Level for Three Sex-race Groups

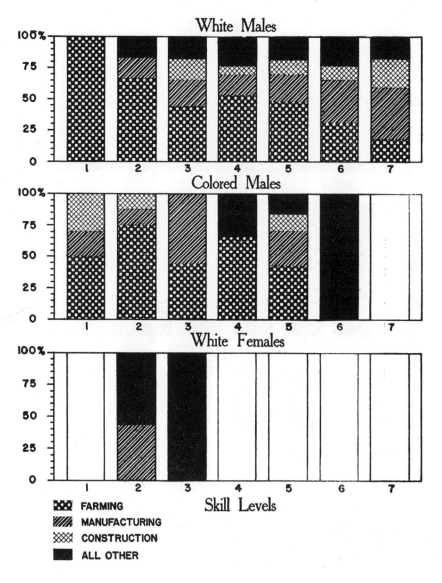

Skill Levels

CHART 44. Number in Each Major Skill Level Group as a Per Cent of Total Employment in Each Skill Level for Three Sex-race Groups

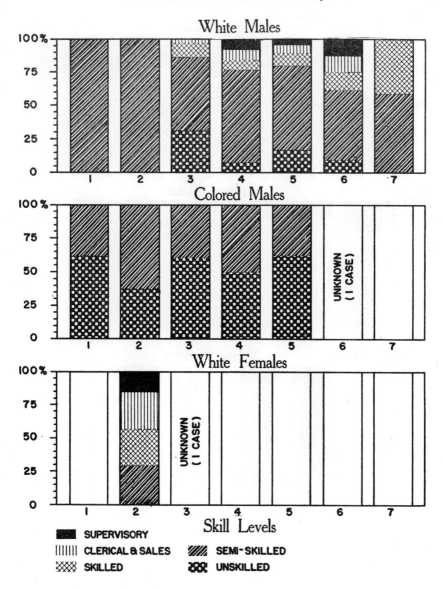

CHART 45. Number in Each Most-recent-job Group as a Per Cent of Total Employment in Each Skill Level for Three Sex-race Groups

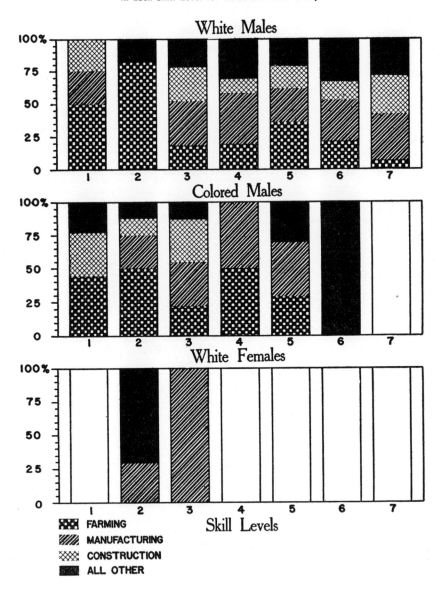

FARMING
MANUFACTURING
CONSTRUCTION
ALL OTHER

CHART 46. Number in Each Most-recent-skill Group as a Per Cent of Total Employment in Each Skill Level for Three Sex-race Groups

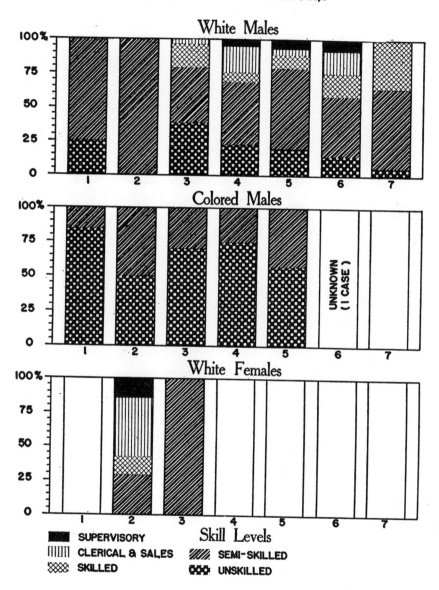

Skill Levels

SUPERVISORY
CLERICAL & SALES   SEMI-SKILLED
SKILLED   UNSKILLED

CHART 47. Number in Each Technical-training Group as a Per Cent of Total Employment
in Each Skill Level for Three Sex-race Groups

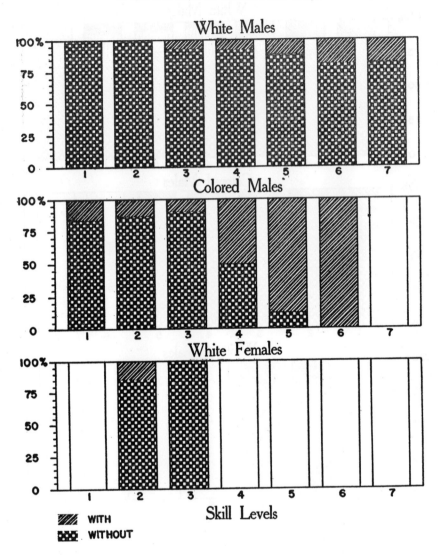

White Males

Colored Males

White Females

Skill Levels

WITH
WITHOUT

APPENDIX D

WEEKLY OUTPUT OF BUSES AND HOURS PER UNIT, PATHFINDER
COACH DIVISION, JULY 1, 1951, TO SEPTEMBER 7, 1952.

WEEK ENDING	UNITS COMPLETED	HOURS PER UNIT
July 1, 1951	12	444.2
July 8, 1951	16	405.0
July 15, 1951	9	920.1
July 22, 1951	10	878.7
July 30, 1951	12	812.8
Aug. 5, 1951	7	1,577.0
Aug. 12, 1951	11	1,201.2
Aug. 19, 1951	33	494.3
Aug. 26, 1951	50	363.6
Sept, 2, 1951	49	372.8
Sept. 9, 1951	25	544.5
Sept. 16, 1951	28	491.7
Sept. 23, 1951	31	462.0
Oct. 1, 1951	48	333.1
Oct. 7, 1951	64	286.5
Oct. 14, 1951	59	283.2
Oct. 21, 1951	49	339.4
Oct. 28, 1951	75	244.3
Nov. 4, 1951	38	412.8
Nov. 11, 1951	67	245.5
Nov. 18 1951	78	224.1
Nov. 25, 1951	43	276.5
Dec, 2, 1951	69	253.1
Dec. 9, 1951	54	260.7
Dec. 16, 1951	66	222.9
Dec. 23, 1951	69	203.4
Dec. 30, 1951	42	210.8
Jan. 6, 1952	38	238.5
Jan. 13, 1952	32	290.7
Jan. 20, 1952	38	239.0
Jan. 27, 1952	41	222.5
Feb. 3, 1952	35	249.7
Feb. 10, 1952	42	207.0
Feb. 17, 1952	35	244.5
Feb. 24, 1952	34	252.1
March 2, 1952	39	216.9
March 9, 1952	33	263.0
March 16, 1952	32	240.8
March 23, 1952	30	203.5
March 30, 1952	35	373.3

WEEK ENDING	UNITS COMPLETED	HOURS PER UNIT
April 6, 1952	24	373.3
April 13, 1952	46	148.8
April 20, 1952	0	0.0
April 27, 1952	24	287.3
May 4, 1952	24	287.3
May 11, 1952	37	214.4
May 18, 1952	37	215.5
May 25, 1952	33	242.9
June 1, 1952	42	194.2
June 8, 1952	42	203.8
June 15, 1952	55	153.6
June 22, 1952	42	215.5
June 29, 1952	17	263.8
July 6, 1952	22	330.0
July 13, 1952	38	242.4
July 20, 1952	44	214.8
July 27, 1952	49	184.6
Aug. 3, 1952	12	793.0
Aug. 10, 1952	48	201.2
Aug. 17, 1952	61	174.1
Aug. 24, 1952	52	223.3
Aug. 31, 1952	60	202.9
Sept. 7, 1952	48	220.4

APPENDIX E

PERFORMANCE MEASURES FOR ADDITIONAL
EMPLOYEE GROUPS

The following groups were not considered important enough to include in Chapter VI of the report but might be of some interest. These groups were those classified by: (1) present residence, (2) veteran status, (3) marital status, (4) technical training.

Absence rates according to present residence are shown in the following table:

ABSENCE RATES

	MISSISSIPPI PRODUCTS		DAY-BRITE	PATHFINDER	
	White Males	Colored Males	White Males	White Males	Colored Males
Local city	3.9	3.1	2.8	1.1	0.4
Local county			2.9	1.1	.6
Contiguous county	4.1	3.4	2.6	1.2	.8
Elsewhere in Mississippi	4.7	*	..	2.1	.1
*Less than 3 cases					

With the exception of the Day-Brite employees living in contiguous counties and the colored males in the Pathfinder plant who resided elsewhere in Mississippi, the expected direct relation between absence rates and distance from the plant was found to prevail among these groups of workers. Several of the colored males in the Pathfinder plant who listed their residence as Greenwood, Mississippi, actually resided in Kosciusko during the work week and returned to Greenwood only for the week-ends.

In the case of one plant a very small advantage in productivity appeared in favor of those whose residence, as of the time of the study, was in rural areas. Their median productivity was 99.8 per cent as against a median productivity of 97.2 per cent for those living in urban areas.

Promotional progress according to present residence is shown in the following table.

PROMOTION RATES

	MISSISSIPPI PRODUCTS		DAY-BRITE
	Skill Level 6 to 5	Skill Level 5 to 4	Helper to Operator
Local city	} 3.9	4.8	2.7
Local county			{ 3.3
Contiguous county	4.2	4.2	
Elsewhere in Mississippi	3.2	2.5	

At Mississippi Products, Inc., the general tendency appeared to be more rapid promotion for those living farther from the plant. In the case of Day-Brite Lighting, Inc., the opposite was true, casting some doubt upon the validity of any generalization that might be made in this connection. It should be noted, however, that the dichotomy used in connection with Day-Brite Lighting, Inc., in actuality constituted a rural-present-residence versus an urban-present-residence breakdown.

Veteran Status. For many of the workers in two plants experience in the armed forces represented a major segment of their lives for a period of time shortly before these studies were made. It would not be surprising to find that military experience or lack of it had a bearing on the success of adaptation to industrial employment. The following table shows the absence rates for veterans and non-veterans:

ABSENCE RATES

	MISSISSIPPI PRODUCTS		DAY-BRITE
	White Males	Colored Males	White Males
Veterans	3.9	4.1	2.5
Non-veterans	4.5	2.8	3.2

The median for colored veterans was considerably in excess of that for non-veterans, indicating that the strict discipline of military life did not carry over into civilian employment. On the other hand, the figures for white males indicated that their military service was followed by lower absenteeism in civilian life.

The following table shows the experience of groups of veterans and non-veterans in output per man-hour:

OUTPUT

	MISSISSIPPI PRODUCTS			DAY-BRITE
	FINISH MILL	HAND BLOCK SANDERS	RUBBERS	
	White Males	*White and Colored Males*	*Colored Males*	*White Males*
Veterans	95.6	97.5	98.4	101.8
Non-veterans	97.3	103.3	101.6	97.4

While in all the measured classifications at Mississippi Products, Inc., non-veterans produced more than veterans, the opposite was true at Day-Brite Lighting, Inc., and to roughly the same extent.

The following table shows the time spent in a lower classification before being promoted to a higher classification for veterans and non-veterans:

PROMOTION RATES

	MISSISSIPPI PRODUCTS		DAY-BRITE
	Skill Level 6 to 5	*Skill Level 5 to 4*	*Helper to Operator*
Veterans	3.6	4.2	5.5
Non-veterans	4.2	5.0	2.3

Again the experience of veterans at Mississippi Products, Inc., and at the Day-Brite plant were opposite, veterans having made the most rapid progress at Mississippi Products, Inc., and non-veterans at Day-Brite Lighting, Inc.

Marital Status. The following table shows absence rates for groups of workers classified by marital status:

ABSENCE RATES

	MISSISSIPPI PRODUCTS		DAY-BRITE	PATHFINDER	
	White Males	*Colored Males*	*White Males*	*White Males*	*Colored Males*
Single	4.1	2.9	2.4	1.3	1.3
Married	3.8	3.3	2.8	1.1	.4

The number of divorced, widowed, and separated was so small that this category is not shown. In two of the three plants, married white males were absent less than single white males as might have been expected in view of the more settled condition of married men. However, at Day-Brite Lighting, Inc., married men were absent more than single men. For the two plants employing colored males, the data were contradictory.

Output by marital status is shown for one plant in the following table:

OUTPUT

| | MISSISSIPPI PRODUCTS | | |
	Finish Mill	Hand Block Sanders	Rubbers
Single	84.0	115.0*	99.0
Married	97.8	100.0	100.4

*Less than 3 cases.

In only two of these cases were there enough men in both categories to invite comparison, and in both of these cases married men produced more than single men.

For only one plant did the data allow a computation of promotional progress according to marital status. The results are shown in the following table:

PROMOTION RATES

| | MISSISSIPPI PRODUCTS | |
	Skill Level 6 to 5	Skill Level 5 to 4
Single	3.8	3.2
Married	3.8	4.8

For one of the promotions, no difference appeared. For the others, at a somewhat higher skill level, single men showed a somewhat more rapid rate of promotion than married men. Perhaps this did not reflect entirely the relative capabilities of the two groups but rather the greater mobility of the single men and therefore greater bargaining power.

Technical Training. In Mississippi there has been hope that specialized technical training would help ease the transition, especially for
the inexperienced, from a non-industrial to an industrial environment. In order to measure the importance of this factor the various
measures of success of transition have been applied to those who had
had technical training outside the public schools and on-the-job
training and to those who had had no such training.

The following table shows absence rates for those with and without
technical training:

ABSENCE RATES

	MISSISSIPPI PRODUCTS		DAY-BRITE	PATHFINDER	
	White Males	Colored Males	White Males	White Males	Colored Males
With technical training	3.7	3.0	3.1	1.1	0.3
All workers	4.0	3.0	..	..	..
Without technical training ..	..	..	2.7	1.2	.7

In two of the three cases of white males, those with technical training were absent less than those without technical training.

The following table shows output for workers with and without
technical training:

OUTPUT

	MISSISSIPPI PRODUCTS	DAY-BRITE
	White and Colored Males	White Males
With technical training	104.5*	More
Without technical training	97.7	Less
*With training in woodworking, cabinet-making, and carpentry.		

It would appear, then, that technical training was helpful in
enabling workers to produce more. However, the fact that workers
most likely to be successful were those who would provide themselves
with technical training might be the explanation.

The following table shows promotional progress for workers with and without technical training:

PROMOTION RATES

	MISSISSIPPI PRODUCTS	DAY-BRITE
	Skill Level 6 to 5	*Helper to Operator*
With technical training	4.5*	2.1
Without technical training	..	3.3
All white males	4.0	..
*With training in woodworking, cabinet-making, and carpentry.		

These figures fail to show any consistent connection between technical training and rate of promotion, as they were contradictory in the cases where there were enough data to permit the analysis.

APPENDIX F

COMPARISON WITH CENSUS DATA

In April, 1950, the median age of the total population was 26.6 years in the South and 32.0 years in the Northeast. Less than one-fourth of the males in the South were fifty years old or over, compared with aproximately one-third in the Northeast. About one-sixth of the females in the South were fifty years old or over, compared with about one-fifth in the Northeast.[1]

The median age of white males in the civilian labor force in the Jackson metropolitan area in April, 1950, was 37.9 years, while that of colored males was 36.6 years.[2] Median ages of Mississippi Products, Inc., employees as of August, 1951, were: white males, 31.2; colored males, 32.3.

The median education of white males 25 years old and over in the Jackson metropolitan area was 12.3 while that of non-white males was 5.7.[3] The median education of Mississippi Products, Inc., employees was: white males, 9.3; colored males, 6.9.

The median age of white males eighteen years old and over in Lee County was 40.1 years.[4] Median age of Day-Brite employees as of March, 1952, was 30.0.

The median education of the white population 25 and over in Lee County was 9.2,[5] and of male population 8.5.[6] Median education of Day-Brite employees was 10.3.

The median age of white males eighteen years old and over in Attala County was 42.1 years, while that of colored males was 38.3 years.[7] Median ages of Pathfinder employees as of November, 1952, were: white males, 31.2; colored males, 32.3.

---

[1]United States Bureau of the Census, *1950 Census of Population, U. S. Summary, Detailed Characteristics* (Washington: Government Printing Office, 1952), II, 374.

[2]United States Bureau of the Census, *1950 Census of Population, Mississippi, Detailed Characteristics*, II, 153-4.

[3]United States Bureau of the Census, *1950 Census of Population, Mississippi, General Characteristics*, II, 149, 150.

[4]*Ibid.*, p. 66.

[5]*Ibid.*, pp. 76, 92.

[6]*Ibid.*, p. 76.

[7]*Ibid.*, p. 60.

The median education of the white population 25 and over in Attala County was 8.6, while that of the non-white population was 5.4. For the entire male population it was 7.7.[8] Median education of Pathfinder employees was: white males, 10.2; colored males, 6.5.

[8]*Ibid.*, pp. 74, 90.

INDEX

absenteeism: age groups, 69, 70; Day-Brite Lighting, Inc., 40; education groups, 73; marital status groups, 141, 142; Mississippi Products, Inc., 22, 24; occupational experience, farming, 80, 81; occupational experience, manufacturing, 84; Pathfinder Coach Division, 54-56; present residence groups, 139; rural-urban background groups, 76, 77; sex-race groups, 68; technical training groups, 143; veteran and non-veteran, 140

accident rates, *see* safety

adaptability of characteristic groups, measures of, 63-67

age groups: absenteeism, 69, 70; layoff rates, 73; output, 71; promotional progress, 71, 72; separation rates, 71, 72

availability of labor: Day-Brite Lighting, Inc., 36-38; general, 90; Mississippi Products, Inc., 17; Pathfinder Coach Division, 46, 48

characteristic groups: adaptability, measures of, 63-67; definition, 12; performance, measures of, 63-67

Day-Brite Lighting, Inc., 34-42, 65, 66, 71-79, 81, 82, 84-87

education groups: absenteeism, 73; layoff rates, 75; output, 74; promotional progress, 75; separation rates, 74

fringe benefits: Day-Brite Lighting, Inc., 36; Mississippi Products, Inc., 18; Pathfinder Coach Division, 47

industrial injuries, *see* safety

labor force: age, compared with census data, 145, 146; education, compared with census data, 145, 146; Day-Brite Lighting, Inc., 38, 39; Mississippi Products, Inc., 20; Pathfinder Coach Division, 48, 49

labor market: Jackson, 14-16; Kosciusko, 34, 35; Tupelo, 43-45

labor recruiting efforts: Day-Brite Lighting, Inc., 37; Mississippi Products, Inc., 16, 17; Pathfinder Coach Division, 46

labor specifications: Day-Brite Lighting, Inc., 37; Mississippi Products, Inc., 17; Pathfinder Coach Division, 47

labor turnover, *see* turnover

labor unions: Day-Brite Lighting, Inc., 36; Mississippi Products, Inc., 19; Pathfinder Coach Division, 48

layoff rates: age groups, 73; educational groups, 75; occupational experience, mfg., 86, 88; rural-urban background groups, 79, 80; sex-race groups, 69

learning period, 20-22, 39

location factors: Day-Brite Lighting, Inc., 35, 36; Mississippi Products, Inc., 16; Pathfinder Coach Division, 45

method of study, 11-13

Mississippi Products, Inc., 14-33, 64, 66, 68, 70-88

occupational experience groups: absenteeism, 80, 81, 84; layoff rates, 86, 88; output, 82, 85, 86; promotional progress, 82, 83, 86, 87; separation rates, 81, 82, 84, 85

output: age groups, 71; Day-Brite Lighting, Inc., 41, 42, 71; education groups,